The
Silence
is
Killing
Me

The
Silence
is
Killing Me

Overcoming
Depression
in a
Faith-based
World

L.S. GILBERT

TATE PUBLISHING
AND ENTERPRISES, LLC

The Silence is Killing Me
Copyright © 2015 by L.S. Gilbert. All rights reserved.

No part of this publication may be reproduced, stored in a retrieval system or transmitted in any way by any means, electronic, mechanical, photocopy, recording or otherwise without the prior permission of the author except as provided by USA copyright law.

Scripture quotations marked (KJV) are taken from the *Holy Bible, King James Version*, Cambridge, 1769. Used by permission. All rights reserved.

Scripture quotations marked (NIV) are taken from the *Holy Bible, New International Version®*, NIV®. Copyright © 1973, 1978, 1984 by Biblica, Inc.™ Used by permission of Zondervan. All rights reserved worldwide. www.zondervan.com

This book is designed to provide accurate and authoritative information with regard to the subject matter covered. This information is given with the understanding that neither the author nor Tate Publishing, LLC is engaged in rendering legal, professional advice. Since the details of your situation are fact dependent, you should additionally seek the services of a competent professional.

The opinions expressed by the author are not necessarily those of Tate Publishing, LLC.

Published by Tate Publishing & Enterprises, LLC
127 E. Trade Center Terrace | Mustang, Oklahoma 73064 USA
1.888.361.9473 | www.tatepublishing.com

Tate Publishing is committed to excellence in the publishing industry. The company reflects the philosophy established by the founders, based on Psalm 68:11,
"The Lord gave the word and great was the company of those who published it."

Book design copyright © 2015 by Tate Publishing, LLC. All rights reserved.
Cover design by Charito Sim
Interior design by Manolito Bastasa

Published in the United States of America

ISBN: 978-1-63418-726-8
1. Religion / Christian Life / Personal Growth
2. Self-Help / Mood Disorders/ Depression
15.08.04

To every believer who has quietly fought for his or her life—you were, and are, never alone.

And to the memory of Brother Warren. Because of you, I gain the will to get out of the bed and try again live again.

Acknowledgments

Before you read any further, I must include this note: this book was not written to expose my family in a negative light or demean them in any way. The personal accounts you will read in these pages are simply my personal truths and my creative perspective on how I once saw my life and the way in which I see it now. I have no life without my family. I have no life without my church or spiritual foundation; therefore, it is improbable that I would be able to share particular parts of my life-journey without including my family. It has been one of the most important pieces in making me who I am.

Family, please know I love you with my heart. I don't believe you knew about my silent struggles. I never had the strength to share them, or maybe, I was too afraid to share them. I trust you will accept my story and the way I have chosen to tell it. Now that I've learned to help myself, I want to help others. Again, I love you, and I hope you can accept and support this testimonial.

Welcome to the conversation. And thank you for listening.

CONTENTS

Introduction 11

PART I

My Struggle

The Silence Is Killing Me 17
It Began at Home 23
A War With Words 31
Functional Dysfunction 41
White Bluff Road 51
Suppressing Depression 59
Tell Me About Your Childhood 67
Unlikely Medicine 73
Intermission: The Bright Side 79
Enough is Enough 85
D-day 95
All Is Well 103

PART II

Your Victory

Prelude to Victory.. 111
Hi, How Are You 115
The Silent Sufferer. 119
A Silent Epidemic. 123
Walls 135
Hurt People Hurt People.. 141
Get Help.. 149
Remember the Word 171
Shower, Shave, and Change. 175
Rest in Peace Now. 181
Notes 189

Introduction

Hi, my name is _____, and I have won a battle with depression. The reason I say *a* battle and not *the* battle is because the war yet continues, and I have to fight consistently to remain in a state of victory. There have been many bouts with depression. Its face changes from time to time, so I don't always immediately recognize it. Its tactics change as well; therefore, I don't readily know how to fight it.

But here I am today with a new tactic of my own: my voice. And as quiet as it may be, it is not silent. The words I write speak louder than the vocal cords ever could, for when and if I am silent, the written word yet remains, bringing power to myself and all who dare to take the chance to read this work.

I have written it in two parts: *my struggle* and *your victory*. Part one tells of my personal story and how I have wrestled with emotional and mental issues. Part two is simply inspiration and encouragement to help you, the reader, live a more victorious life free of mental distresses. I am well aware that I am breaking some secret code by speaking up about this issue, and perhaps I will be stoned for even suggesting that any *Christian* could be dealing with issues in his or her mind. Thank you for choosing to join the discussion.

I have reached this conclusion: I'll not allow myself to die quietly on the backstage of life. Depression softly kills, sucking the life out of every heart that feels broken, of every soul that feels forsaken, of every love that's been betrayed. Today, I pull back the curtains. Depression must take its final bow—it's time for *my* show to begin.

My name is Liconya. I am a Christian who battles with depression. The silence is killing me. So, today I speak, if for no other reason than to live.

*Thanks to the Almighty,
I am no longer sleepwalking through life.*

—Stanley "Tookie" Williams

Part I

MY STRUGGLE

*It was good for me
that I have been afflicted;
that I might learn thy statutes.*

—Psalm 119:71

THE SILENCE IS KILLING ME

I GREW UP living a pretty sheltered life. Granted I didn't know that it was sheltered until I was older, and someone from the outside told me that that was my "problem." Okay, so I lacked social skills. I didn't know how to relate to people on a personal level. Truth is I didn't want to relate to them on a personal level. I wanted to be left alone: meet, greet, say good-bye. There was nothing else necessary. Where had I learned to be so short with people? Why didn't I care to get to know anyone past learning his or her name? Surely, my wonderful *Christian* upbringing had prepared me to love on all levels and treat everyone with respect. (If you sensed cynicism in that last remark, perhaps you're right.)

I spent quite a bit of time in church. I suppose my family faithfully began attending when I was about four years old after my mom moved us to North Florida. Church would become my world. When people asked what it was I did for fun, I would innocently say, "Go to church." That, of course, was alongside reading and traveling. Church was an outlet for the most part. Now that I'm older, I can't say how much of anything else it was for me. It simply was the one place to which I knew I'd be going every Sunday, Wednesday, and Friday (with choir rehearsal and church cleaning on Saturday) until I was old enough to have the nerve to escape. I will admit church became *my* choice after a while. No one had to make me go. Eventually, someone would have to make me stay but not for obvious reasons.

Talking about how or, perhaps I should say, where I grew up doesn't hold as much importance as I would like. It doesn't speak of my imperfections. And it ignores my humanity. I realize that I was never allowed to be human. I was groomed to try all things "by the spirit" and live "in the spirit" and ignore the "flesh"—as if a person could really do that—and resist the devil at all costs. There was no "devil's music." There was no use of profanity. There was no drinking of alcohol, no smoking of cigarettes, no lying, no cheating, no stealing. *No nothing*. The Ten Commandments—those in the Bible and the made-up ones—were to be an everyday, ever-ready guide to eternal life, and anyone who thought to divert from these "laws" were surely seeking to someday burn in hell.

I suppose, at many times, I was the captain of that ship. Having made the choice to lie, cheat *and* steal on more than one occasion surely made me a sinner worthy of stoning. So often, the stones were cast by he who was unworthy—especially when he cast them for all of the wrong reasons. I remember quite vividly a time when I was beaten for telling the truth. That moment convinced me that there was no reward for honesty. Am I blaming the suspect for every lie I told from that moment on? No. But I guess it does identify the root of a problem with which I once flirted quite often.

Anyhow, that's neither here nor there. I write in this moment because I felt inclined to do so. Lying in bed trying to filter through my thoughts of how I will strategize my survival, this thought comes to mind, *The silence is killing me.* You see, in church, I was taught to keep it to myself, blame it on the devil—but give him no credit—and when the trial is done, give glory to God. But you dare not speak of the trouble you see, or the pain you feel, or the love you long for, or your desire to leave your family, your church *or* your God. You dare not talk of the struggles you have in the midnight hour. Or the ones you have in the middle of the day. You better not talk of being disturbed in your mind. Don't you know God has given you perfect peace? So if you've no peace, you must not be a servant of God. Choosing to talk about it rather than pray (to God) about it was somehow a sin in and of itself. And if that is the case, I find myself wanting to sin more and more because I can no longer *not* talk about it. I can no longer choose to not talk about the things that silently tear at my core as I continue to try and live life with a smile so pastel I could make a doll baby jealous. The hurt, the pain, the fears of failure, success, and love—I want to talk about what bothers me about life, about death, about sex, about marriage. I want to discuss the very possible idea that God just might not exist. I want to be able to come to the person who claims to care about me and tell him or her about my thoughts of suicide. I want to discuss the effects of the war in Afghanistan. I want to talk about how I hated that I grew up in church. I want to yell. I want to scream. I want to live. I want to love. And I want to do it all without being stoned for it and without fear, for if I am not able to speak, the voice I once had will die and ultimately so will I.

> *O Lord my God, I cried unto thee,*
> *and thou hast healed me.*

—Psalm 30:2

As many things may be holding me back
at this moment in time,
I shall not refrain from
living life to its fullest,
as it is rapidly drawing to a close.
Even though I may feel
that I'm not a part of the world
and yet in it—
not a part of a family,
but still yet with it.
I shall gradually finish my course—
for I have almost learned to love again.

—*Only God Can Judge Me* (1999)

It Began at Home

I BELIEVE I was a teenager when I began to faithfully write in a journal. My first journal was a gift given by a very close friend of the family. She was the only person I would actually talk to about how I was feeling sometimes, but even with her, I didn't share everything.

I started writing poetry when I was about nine years old. I was in the third grade. I spent many years writing for pleasure. And then, one day, I began writing for pain. And that's how I would begin keeping the journal. I suppose my emotions could no longer be confined to the rhyming of every other line and four-line stanzas. I needed more ink, and I needed more paper because my heart began to talk more often and much louder than I would have ever thought to allow. It was not privy to such freedom, and I fought to keep it that way. Evidently, that is a fight I lost.

I can remember when I began to shut down on the world around me, but I can't quite remember the reason why. Maybe I was tired of being called *ugly*. Maybe I was tired of struggling with my secret sins. Maybe I just wanted to fit in for a change. I don't really know. I just know the world around me had begun to change, and like the man who washed off the mud Jesus had put on his eyes, I began to see men as trees. Unlike the man, however, I had no strength to go and wash my eyes again.

I was growing up. Me and my siblings had very distinct personalities, and at times, I felt that maybe I was adopted. I don't know why I would feel so out of place. Surely, my parents loved me just as much as they did my brother and sister, and they wanted what was best for us all. There were, perhaps, many times when I felt like I wanted to run away. And I tried, but I can assure you the task was only fully carried out in my mind. Later it made for a wonderful journal entry. What's crazy is I honestly believe my parents wouldn't have noticed I was gone. They wouldn't have believed it if I had told them. And maybe, they really wouldn't have cared. The extent of their concern would have only been defined by their instruction to go into the room and pray, which simply meant to call on the name of Jesus until I "felt something."

Considering those things, I knew I wanted something more. I don't know if I wanted something more from myself or from my family, but I wanted more. I wanted things to be different. I wanted things to change. If I had to be a "church girl," I wanted to be a church girl who said the right things, did the right things even when no one else was watching. I was a disgruntled girl—victorious in the light but defeated in the shadows. Eventually, the dysfunction would show up and make a statement, and I would find myself embarrassed and too far gone to find a way to fix it.

I Cried for More

Many years went by before I was able to tell someone what I needed. The things I needed had once been wants, simple desires, which no one cared to supply. So then, they became necessary for me or else I would surely die. For the most part, I just needed someone to talk to. The family friend was cool. The journal was a blessing. And the poetry was God's way of giving me a piece of Himself. At some point though, even the poetry would not be enough. I needed a real-life person. *I wanted my mother*. And she was there, I just did not know how to ask her for more of herself, and that pained me.

Aside from that, I realized that I also wanted a different kind of relationship with God. The preacher preached sermon after sermon about how I should live in order to rid myself of the fate of hell. And that would be my goal, *do not go to hell*. (Heaven seemed like such a better place for which to strive, but hey, what do I know.) I remember silently craving a worship experience. I would eventually suppress this urge for a "worship experience," but I wrote about it in that journal. And years afterward, it was that journal that reminded me of such desires.

So I wanted more God. And I wanted more love.

I wanted to feel love. I wanted to talk about it. I wanted to share it with others. So many times, I felt like it was my responsibility to lead my own way. It was as if I had been tried—and approved—well before I knew it and was forced to live up to some unknown standard. So I cried out for help. A joke of some sort was often the disguise for my cries. And when no one would get it, I chose to retreat like an army that was sure it had lost yet another battle. There was often no hope to fight another day. But I did.

I can remember being so afraid to talk that I would leave notes for my mom on the counter even when I needed things as simple as her signature on a permission slip. One day I would leave a note on the counter, and she would let me know how she felt about it. Needless to say, that was the last note I would leave on the counter.

Aggghhhhh! The screams inside my mind. How I wish I could have had the strength to articulate with my mouth the things I felt inside of my heart. But fear would win every time, and I would retire to my pen and paper and write in hopes to redeem myself of the pain: "The Things I Cannot Change," "Lonely Teardrops," "This is How I Feel,"

"Only God Can Judge Me." The list goes on. And the pain? Well, it intended to leave, but it more than overstayed its welcome. Eventually it would leave though, but not until quite a few years would pass and many tears would be cried. I spent many years crying, and I'm almost sure nobody knew. I had long since stop crying in front of my family because when I cried, my stepdad would say I was nothing but a barrel of water. That would actually hurt my feelings, so I learned to stop crying. I didn't want people to view me as weak. I would learn to not express my feelings. I would never cry in front of people again.

So maybe the moment I was told to stop crying was the start of me crying out for more. It made me stronger, but not for long. And eventually, it made me needy. Most people thought I was strong, but there were some who dared to see past my "rough exterior" and conclude that I really did have a heart. People would always tell me—and some still tell me now—that I need to stop being so "hard" and just relax. I'm not really so hard, but it's hard to relax when tension is all that has been known for the past twenty years.

Funny how I am now learning how to cry. The things I used to cry *for* are now a part of my life, and everything I refused to cry *about* then is making its way to the surface. I cry now. Both tears of joy and tears of sorrow. The joy in all of that is that I now know the difference, and I recognize that, either way, tears are *not* bad.

I bet there were at least a few people who looked at me and figured I was the product of a near-perfect home. I did well in school (up until a certain point). My parents took me to church every week, and I was well on my way to being a leader. My school friends didn't always understand me, my teachers loved me, and there was no heaven the people at church weren't willing to put me in. Even with that, I was growing into this heartless person because I was being teased at school, misunderstood at home, and I was growing weary of the mirage of church into which I was thrown on a weekly basis in order to convince me that everything would be all right as I incessantly repented of sins not even committed and praised a God I wasn't allowed to question.

Am I blaming my family (or my God) for my issues? Not exactly. But if I am to walk in a deliverance I've fought hard to obtain, it is necessary that I identify the roots of malfunction that have been implanted in my life. I've spent quality time attempting to understand myself so that I may be a better person, a better daughter, a better friend, a better Christian, and someday make some man happy because I am a better wife. The word scars, the neglect, the silent tears. All of these things—along with so many others—helped to make me the person I have become today. Though the issues I had, or perhaps still have, began at home, I understand that I have the power to overcome those things. So I continue to cry out for more even in my adult life because I insist on being a better *me*. The little girl has had her chance to speak. She may be silent, but she is not dead. She watches in the shadows as I become the dream she had so many years ago.

I leave home so that I may fully grow.

> *When my father and my mother forsake me,*
> *then the Lord will take me up.*
>
> —Psalm 27:10

> *I cried unto God with my voice, even unto God*
> *with my voice; and he gave ear unto me.*
>
> —Psalm 77:1

The first time she questioned me of assumed crime
I spoke nothing but the truth
but somehow in honesty's moment
I became a troubled youth…
And all this time I've had a problem
with opening my heart.
It's kind of hard to trust[again]
when I never had the chance to start.
I suppose the problem could lie within me—
deep inside there's a troubled youth
who's holding on to a grudge
all because she told the truth.
And now a note to self:
Honesty is only good enough to get you into heaven.

—Excerpt from *The Grudge*

A War With Words

I T WAS SOME time in 2008. I received a certified letter in the mail from the United States Army. It was orders to *die*. Okay, well, the paperwork did not exactly read that way, but it may as well could have. There was a letter and a set of orders sending me to Afghanistan to fight in a war that I secretly didn't support or believe in. I began to cry as I read my fate. I had heard that I might be called to active duty, but it wasn't real until that moment.

As the time drew closer for me to leave my home for a year, I did my best to ignore the fact that I was going to *war*. People around me seemed to make it their business to remind me of the task. They would ask how I felt and if I was afraid. Somehow, I wasn't. And that was the truth. I was going to a land that was not my home. I would have a weapon in tow—which would also become my bunkmate—and I would have to learn to adjust to a temporary environment that would permanently change me.

The fear that I may have had had nothing to do with the fact that the risk of death would drastically increase for me the moment I stepped foot on that Afghan soil. I understood the risks. They were the same *American* risks; however, more bold, more real, less predictable. The life I had had become more precious in an instant, and that precious feeling grew every day I was awakened by a boom in the middle of the night or the sunrise just beyond the cliffs of the mountains. And though I had my "fearful" moments, I was unafraid of *that* war, maybe because, in some way, it had nothing to do with me.

Now that I have had a couple of years to sit back, reflect, recollect, and readjust I can't help but to think that my fearlessness of that war was merely a disguise for the fear I was already facing. I was in my own war and had been for years. I was in the army now—*war was my job*. But before soldiering ever became a part of my life, I had been trying to learn how to fight. The enemy was me, and I was always in the line of fire, resting in enemy territory as if it were my home.

Going to war for the country caused me to forget about my own war. It was no longer about me. There would be fellow soldiers—and my friends and family—who would need me to be healthy in my body *and* my mind. So I displaced myself from myself in order to survive. What I failed to realize was that life would soon come back to "normal," and

I would have to learn to fight again, would have to learn the keys to survival in my own home, in my own mind. My life, this time, was dependent upon it.

It is very easy, almost too easy, to get away with murdering the self when the choice has been made to live life alone. Suicide would be too quick. Torture would take too long. Execution would be unjustified. So murder it is. At least that way I could somehow talk to myself as I attempt to rid myself of myself. *And that ain't no easy thing.* (Trying to commit the act is one thing; getting away with it is another.) It takes time to convince yourself that your life is not worth living. It takes the right people saying a lot of the wrong things, and you believing those things. Oddly enough, the *wrong* people can say those same things, and those things mean nothing until *the right people confirm them*. It takes spending a lot of quality time convincing the self that what everyone else is saying about you is the right thing, and what you believe about yourself is merely a dream. He said, she said—the beginning of war.

I Can Hear You

I suppose you never realize that it is a war you're in until the battles prove themselves to be many. One after another, after another, and you find yourself in war. The battles start off small. And generally, they have no real meaning until you wake up one day and notice the consistency of the matter. I went through this yesterday. Why does this keep happening? Why is everybody always picking on me? The thoughts build upon themselves. You recognize that it's you against the world. War has been declared against you, and finally, you acknowledge the truth and reluctantly begin to fight. You never did accept the challenge.

I believe my first of many battles began on the playground or maybe on the school bus. The exact location may not be so important, considering the keywords *playground* and *school bus*. From my hair and teeth to my clothes and shoes, I was the brunt of many jokes (for many years). I would learn to defend myself against even the people who had nothing to say. I suppose I was some kind of justified bully, putting fear in people before they could get to me. I was only hurt, offended, challenged by the people who were seemingly stronger than me. Perhaps they could smell my fear. Adults were the only people I could trust. Little did I know, some of them would one day betray me too.

Ugly was the word used to describe me all too often, and I never believed it to be true until I heard it from people I cared about. *Ugly?* I'm not even sure I knew exactly what it meant the first time I heard the word. I just knew it wasn't good. At first, you hear things in whispers. Then your ears perk up, and you hear things so clear that you begin to hear with your heart. Hurt feelings emerge, and you begin to defend yourself while it is light. But when darkness comes, you are a different person. In the day, you are bold, courageous, and strong—no one on that school bus will get to you today. But at night, when your parents have sent you to bed, you begin to remember all of the things people said—at school *and* at home—and you hope tomorrow will not repeat itself.

Tomorrow? If only it was all there was to worry about. Years pass but you learn to cope, or at least you think you learn, until someone new comes along to rip the scab from a wound that has refused to fully heal.

But you get through it. You always do. As the years pass, you try to learn to trust. You find avenues for which to expose yourself. You sing, you write, you create anything to help you find your own worth and only hope that someone else can see it too. I had long since learned there was no hope in my natural beauty. As far as *it* was concerned, it did not exist for me. I had heard what had been said, *I was ugly*. But in my poetry, in my journal, in my drawings, there was beauty. My mind was a Garden of Eden, a meadow filled with beauty, which could only be seen in one's imagination: it was far too precious for the wildest dream. And when I engulfed myself in those things, I was no longer the person I had heard others describe, and for just a moment, people could get a chance to see the *real* me, past my skin tone, past the buckteeth. Past the not-so-pretty face and the old-lady ways, I became an artist. There was respect for my beautiful mind.

The thing about the mind though is that it has the tendency to malfunction. And after you learn to think with the mind (and the heart), you cannot afford malfunction. I'm not so sure I was supposed to hear everything that was ever said about me. Maybe people did not always intend for me to hear, but I did. I'm not so sure they always intended for me to suffer, but I did. I gained a boost of confidence when I learned to proclaim that sticks and stones might break my bones, but words will never hurt me. The first few times I said it, it was truth, and I believed it. Eventually, when I said it, it would be a lie, although I still wanted to believe it. I don't believe I've ever been attacked with a stick or a stone, but who needs either of those things when words are out there for the taking, to be used any way anyone pleases. Words. Hurt.

If I could have ever known the relentless life that ill words could have, perhaps I would have taken a moment to learn how to process the negative things I heard in a seemingly more positive way. That is what's supposed to happen, right? Someone says you'll never amount to anything; you prove them wrong by becoming everything you set out to do. Someone calls you stupid or dumb; you begin to read more, study harder and allow your grades to talk for you. Someone calls you black and ugly; you smile a broader smile and hold your head a little higher because there is something about you that keeps getting their attention. (And smile, because it finally makes sense.)

Sure, I got some pretty good poetry out of the deal, but the day did come when that wasn't enough anymore. Writing in a journal was no longer an outlet of fulfillment. And songs of joy would eventually become the blues. So what happens when the things you turned to for comfort, for beauty, are no longer at your disposal? You get up—eventually—and you finally go to that mirror that you make every effort to avoid, even when you're brushing your teeth or doing your hair. You look at yourself, albeit through tears, and somehow talk to yourself and make an effort to counteract every negative thing that's been said about you and that you've adopted as truth for yourself. And that is what you do as long as it takes to get yourself to see you as you ought.

He said what he said. She said what she said. But what do *you* say? Just like you were able to hear what others have said—and you believed it—I encourage you to say some things and believe it. Find strength and words of encouragement through the Bible. Surround yourself with people who believe in you and who can see your potential to become great. (I'm a witness that there's at least one person God has assigned to our lives for that very purpose.) Read a good book. Sing a happy song. Live a full life. Why come home proud to have survived the war if you're only going to return and continue to be afraid to live? *This has been a conversation with myself.*

The biggest, most important war any man will ever have to fight is the war within him. The Apostle Paul described the "war within" very distinctly. He adamantly says how there is a war within him, and that war causes him to do wrong when he knows he has a desire to do right. As long as we're on this earth, war is inevitable. The war does not have to be unto death. It is possible to enjoy life even in the midst of war. (I would like to think I'm enjoying peacetime in this moment.) The battles that we have to face come to us for different reasons, and half the time, the reasons will remain unclear and will seem absolutely pointless. My battles began with words, and oftentimes, words are still the fuel. Funny how the weapon that has been used to destroy me has been the very weapon that has been used to protect me. Words have sustained me, they've been my resuscitation from the time I was a little girl, even until now. And they will live after I am gone.

Though my mouth sometimes gets me in trouble, I have come to learn the importance of saying the right thing. I realize that there is no way for me to know what every person could be dealing with in his or her personal life when we cross paths. There may very well be a little girl inside of that woman who has been waiting on someone to say something different for a change. As superficial as it could seem, every woman wants to hear from someone else that she is beautiful, not just on the inside, but the outside as well. Every man wants to hear from someone else that he is a great man and has some importance in the world. Words can hurt, but they also have the power to heal. If I am a wounded warrior, I have less effect than I could have if I were fully healthy. I've learned that I must be a part of my own healing—and spread the word.

There is a part of me that wakes up every day hoping that it will be the day that I will choose to be consistent with myself. I need to look in the mirror like I did that one time and see beauty. And I need to strive to see it every day until it is beauty the mirror sees when it shows me a reflection. Through the words spoken that caused pain of the past, for the words that will bring healing to my present and future, I realize that I owe it to myself to live healed. I will. That's my word. Word is bond.

I do not understand what I do.
For what I want to do I do not do,
but what I hate I do…
For I know that good itself does not dwell in me,
that is, in my sinful nature.
For I have the desire to do what is good,
but I cannot carry it out.

—Romans 7:15, 18 (NIV)

Functional Dysfunction

I DIDN'T REALLY choose to write this book. I guess someone could say it kind of chose me. I would never care to tell particular details of my life, especially if it means disclosing what would appear to be the dark truth that is *depression*. The idea for this book came from out of nowhere. I was newly unemployed and was lying in my bed (on what was a workday a week prior) and was thinking, with my eyes closed. And the title came to me very clear. I grabbed my laptop and began to type.

I'm not so sure I cared to talk about myself or my family in such a way as to bring shame or embarrassment. I guess, for me, the mission here is to get completely healed and to help someone along the way. If healing is to be acquired, I guess I must talk about some things that may not be too comfortable. This leads to the address of this chapter: *dysfunction*.

I'm not a drinker, and gratefully, I didn't grow up in a house where alcohol was abused, or welcomed for that matter. But I have heard about functional alcoholics. A person drinks and drinks and knows he has a problem but has somehow managed to master the ability to carry on with his normal activities as if he were sober. It is clear that the dysfunction of alcoholism is present, but for this person, it is not acceptable to *be* an alcoholic; therefore, he must maintain that he is well by attempting to continue to function as normal. I don't believe I've ever seen someone attempt this feat, but I can only imagine how tired (and relieved) he must be once he is in the confines of his home and realizes he has succeeded once again. He lives with a *functional* dysfunction.

Although alcoholism isn't my plight, I can identify with the sickness of dysfunction. And it may not be a *sickness* in the eyes of most other people, but that is what it has become to me. In fact, it may be more like a disease, because dysfunction has a way of showing up in one area of life and spreading into others. Before long, it incapacitates everything a person hopes to do, and she will either have to feed the dysfunction or try to make it without it. I eventually learned how to function with the dysfunction. It was just easier that way, or at least it seemed to be. I figured there was no use in fighting it and chose to accept the truth (at the time) that that's just the way things were for me. It was my normal and it would be my normal, until one day I went to church and heard a sermon titled, "Dysfunctional Families."

Whose Family? Not Mine!

Praise and worship offered. Announcements made (during offering time). Choir sang. Then, the sermon. This was the way of the Sunday morning worship service. I knew the pastor or whoever was speaking that morning would have something thought-provoking to share with the congregation. Very few times did I feel like the *messenger* was talking to me, but this Sunday was different. The pastor graced the pulpit. Read the sermon text, which, to my memory was selected verses from 2 Samuel 13, tells the story of David's son Amnon, who raped Tamar, his sister, which was an issue never properly handled. After a short prelude, the pastor spoke his sermon title: Dysfunctional Families. *Dun-dun-dun*—I silently took deep breaths as I felt my heart do its infamous he-must-be-talking-about-me dive into the pit of my stomach. There was no way *my* family was dysfunctional. We were a church-going, faithful-to-the-work, train-up-a-child-in-the-way-it-should-go religious kind of family who had its place at the pastor's table and would surely have a place at God's table as well. Perhaps I'm putting a lot on it in this moment, but for the sake of the truth, that *is* my truth. Because we were in church (usually more than we were at home), I would have never thought to think that my family was dysfunctional. Sure, we had our problems—what family doesn't?—but we didn't usually talk about them. *Dysfunction*. We simply exercised our faith and took it to the Lord in prayer. Dysfunction. And by prayer, I simply mean that I was instructed to call on the name of Jesus over and over again—and loudly—and ask Him to forgive me. Need I say dysfunction? And I shouldn't neglect my siblings in this moment; they had to call Jesus's name too. Oftentimes though, I didn't feel He was listening, much less coming to my aid. Why else would I need to say His name so many times? *Maybe He was as tired of me calling His name as I was.* As a child, I was sure there was more, and Jesus was not hard of hearing.

Anyhow, the crux of the sermon was not simply about Amnon's cruel violation of his sister's virtue; it was also the mishandling of the situation on David's part, and Absalom's desire to vindicate his sister's virtue. Absalom's hate for Amnon fueled his desire to have him killed. Why did Absalom feel it necessary to take matters into his own hands? Did he not trust David's ability to rectify the situation as a father should? The Bible says David was "very wroth" when he heard of the ill deed (v. 21). Okay, so he was angry. But what did he *do* about it? Sometimes I miss things when I read the Bible, but I don't see where David did anything. Oh, how the issues ensue.

And isn't that how it goes for many people? Children have issues (and passions) that their parents once had or have, but they are never taught how to tame those passions.

At the very least, David should have gathered his family together to pray, worship, write a psalm, or whatever it is he practiced that made him a man after God's heart. David dropped the ball on this one. And maybe, Absalom could have handled the situation (very) differently—but then we'd not have the example to live by. Thanks, David.

No one stripped me of my virtue. My brother did not put a hit out on any of my other siblings. But there is the guilt of silence. I wonder what salvation I could have experienced before now if at least one person would have taken the time to talk with me, *to* me, about life—about *anything*. How many times have you reached a destination and learned that there was a different route, a better route from the person who was on the journey with you? I would imagine it's like being blind and having an escort, someone who can see just fine, but he lets you go on your way as if you can see where you're going. And I shake my head in this moment at the thought of someone watching me walk into a wall that he knew was there but refused to give a warning. Oh, the bruises I have perhaps sustained that I did not have to.

Why does it seem like there are secrets? Sometimes our parents don't know what to tell us. They just know they want to save us, protect us from those things that are unknown to us. And if you were anything like me when I was a teenager, you were pretty quiet, standoffish, sneaky, and kept things to yourself. You were convinced your parents were not concerned, and eventually they were just going to tell you to *pray about it*. And who's interested in that, right? All you know is that success in life—not academically, financially, or even socially, but in life—seems to be one big secret that will not be disclosed until you spend a good forty years wandering in the wilderness. And before long, you find yourself at a crossroads, wondering where you went wrong and what happened to everybody who was apparently once a part of your team. You don't know why you act the way you do, why you keep giving in to certain things, why you let people take advantage of you, why you don't show affection, why you despise being touched by other people. Why? Why? *Why!*

I will not call your family dysfunctional. I don't care to label mine either; however, I do believe every family has its issues. Greater than that, I believe some of the issues we may deal with in our adult lives stem from disregarded, unspoken, ill-attended issues from childhood and/or family. Hearing this sermon is what caused the alarm to sound for me. *I was dysfunctional.*

The Blame Game

Well, whose fault is it anyway? I mean I had to blame somebody, right? I, by default, picked my mother. We are so much alike. She didn't talk much, and at some point, I assumed that was how I was supposed to be. I kept people out. And by *kept them out*, I mean I had security for the security guarding my life. My business was my business, and anything I did had really nothing to do with anyone else. Sure, there were moments when I included people. Most of those moments happened at church, but they were moments nonetheless. I allowed people to share my academic feats. I shared my poetry. I sang in the choir. That was it to life, and outside of that, no one needed to inquire anything of me. I was my mother's daughter, and I was proud of the way I was—at least for a while.

I suppose I could have blamed my biological dad. I mean, wasn't it his fault that I was so despondent to other male figures in my life? My poor stepfather: I can only imagine how I made him feel for at least the first few years of his and my mom's marriage. I don't know if I ever told him, but I probably often reminded him in some other ways that he was not my daddy. But my dad was not there. Did he abandon me? I can't say that, especially since he made guest appearances from time to time throughout my childhood. But maybe he is the reason why I don't let people in because eventually they will love me, then leave.

I smile right now because I realize the list could perhaps go on for a few more paragraphs. But I can't blame anyone for the way I am or the way I *was*. When I do an evaluation, I try to pinpoint what series of events could perhaps have led to my shutdown and taught me how to function with dysfunction. Something happened, or someone did something at some point that interrupted the flow of my heart. I stopped trusting, I stopped loving, I stopped caring. I didn't want it to be anyone else's problem because it was a hard problem for me, and I just couldn't bear the idea of someone else feeling that way. I was a sad child. I was a hurting child. I wanted someone to talk to me. I wanted someone to understand me. It seemed no one did unless I was singing a song, reciting a poem, making the honor roll, staying out of (visible) trouble. I played the part well and did so until the day I heard that sermon.

From that moment, I was determined to *fix* myself. It was not my mother's problem. It was not my father's *or* stepfather's problem. It was not the problem of my sister or the problem of the church. (Yeah, I know that is an erroneous statement to make.) I was an adult now, and in order to properly function as one, I would need to stop functionally dysfunctioning. At this point, if I were going to blame anyone, I would have to turn my finger to myself. Besides, I was so tired of trying to drive forward with the car stuck in neutral. Although that was the only surefire way to know my emotions went in the direction of which I wanted them to go or nowhere at all. Yeah. You see how that turned out.

There is a happy ending. I no longer love from a place of hurt. And although I'm (very) hesitant to trust, I at least have learned how to trust first from a place of innocence rather than deeming someone guilty, until he or she proves to be innocent. I'm still quite cautious, but I am functional. I get a little afraid sometimes, but I am functional. Sometimes it hurts to learn the truth, but I seek to remain functional. Wrapped up in all of the reasons why Jesus died on the Cross is the reason of my functionality. Really, Christ died for my dysfunctions: the sin, the anger, the harvested hurt, the resuscitated pain, the distrust, the mishandled love. He died for it all.

All these problems combining to make one big issue
makes me want to see a big tree and hit it,
urges me to stand on the edge and jump
but God convinces me to forget it…

—Excerpt from "Lord Get Me Out of This"

WHITE BLUFF ROAD

I TRAVELED THIS road often. As a matter of fact, I lived in an apartment complex on this road. At the time, it was one of the major roads in Savannah, GA. I learned to use it as an alternative to the busier Abercorn Street, and soon it would become the anticipated place of my future demise. I was contemplating suicide.

There was a big oak tree, or at least I assume it was an oak tree, in the median. It seemed to be the perfect tree for the park or maybe a huge back yard. It was a huge tree with a trunk seemingly twice the size of other trees which occupied the medians along White Bluff Road. It caught my eye with every commute (specifically to church). And it was perfect.

Perhaps I'd not even have a plan if it weren't for that tree. It was the focal point of my picture, the thesis of my paper. All other details would evolve around it. And it was no complicated plan. The tree was near the edge of the median and therefore, closer to the road, riding east. (Or maybe it was west. My sense of direction was always off in Savannah.) Anyhow, the plan was as simple as me bending over to pick something up off the floorboard of the car at just the right moment—no, it was not enough to just simply take my eyes off the road—and somehow veer to the left just enough only to look up (a moment too late) and crash head-on into that tree. I don't know why it had to be *that* one, but it was the chosen one, and I was committed to it.

Why Suicide?

Honestly, I don't know. But I will say this: it seemed like a good idea at the time. All catchphrases aside, I didn't know what was going on or why I felt so unhappy. I had a job, I was going to church, I was enjoying living in my very first apartment. I was in a relationship. Wait—maybe that was it. I was not yet back in school, but I would be soon. I had everything I needed to be *happy*. I was miserable inside though. I always felt like I was trying to please other people. I felt like I was not good enough for some people. I had long since begun to feel like my parents really didn't want me around. After all, I was still in Savannah at my mother's insistence—a conversation we had had before the leasing of the apartment—that it was not time for me to return home. Wait, I'm blaming again, aren't I? And then there was the experience I was having at church. It was different from what I was accustomed to, but it was absolutely what I needed. It was what I had been longing to experience. So I don't know what was *wrong*.

I remember being so frustrated in my relationship that I would request to take "space" often. In retrospect, I believe I took space about six times over the course of two years. I remember there being unfamiliar temptations, and I would write the guy off as *the one* for me. I remember feeling unhappy with some of the other choices I had made, and I was beginning to feel like I was not even good enough for myself. I remember wanting to feel my mother's love in a way that said more than "I'm your mother." I needed it to say "I'm your mother, and I love you." I wanted that. I needed that. I'm still unsure of how suicide ever became an option, but it was *the* option. For at least one moment, I had made a subconscious decision to no longer take my burdens to God. I was going to take them to the grave. After all, I didn't have any *real* issues. I didn't even know what to tell God. I didn't know how to describe it to anyone else, so I did what I did best and kept how and what I was feeling to myself. Eventually, my thoughts turned into thoughts of suicide. It seems I had long since been tired. I was tired of performing. I was tired of my functional dysfunction. I was just tired. I had lived a life in church, but for what? I had tried my best in school, but for what? The recent years had proven that I was a failure, and everything I had done to be whatever I hoped I'd be was in vain and now a bonfire filled with lofty pursuits.

And then there was that man. Really? I had the nerve to accept someone into my life when I know I only had an extreme inability to love anything, anybody who could do me harm? Talk about taking chances. I honestly believed he was the one. And nothing, not even taking care of my firstborn nephew the year prior—which was the beginning of God's lessons in retraining my heart to love—prepared me to give my heart, much less my body, to a man. It was too much. I had not yet dealt with the things that I needed to work on in my own life, and there's no way I would trust this man enough to *fix* me.

Needless to say, I didn't even know I was broken. But I was. But who would I tell? Who could I tell who was not going to steer me in the direction of the nearest altar, encourage me to lift my hands in surrender, and give my burdens to God? What's funny is, I thought God's reaction would be similar, so I didn't tell Him either—at least not at first.

In the Apartment on White Bluff Road

Although it may have been encouraged at some point or another, I didn't grow up having many church services in my home. I didn't worship at home. My brother and sister and I played church, but aside from calling on Jesus 'til I felt something, there was no conjuring of God's presence in the home. That was something I naturally assumed was intended for the sanctuary, with other people, and (particularly) on a Sunday. But because of my recent experiences in church at that time, I was learning to worship God at home. Granted, during this time however, I was kind of shut down on the process altogether. Yeah, it's just not guards against people with me; even God gets put out when I am encased by my fears and emotions. But He would trespass into my pity party like He did to Elijah when he was under the juniper tree, and choose to strengthen me, whether I wanted to be strengthened or not.

I remember it quite vividly. I was in the kitchen cooking or preparing to cook. I was frustrated, and knowing me, I was having a good conversation about it with myself out loud. I don't know what I did or didn't do, but at some point between me fussing at someone who was not there (everyone else) or someone who was just choosing not to listen (myself) and placing food in the frying pan I had placed on the stove, the pan caught on fire. I grabbed it quickly and threw it into the kitchen sink. Once the fire was out, I began to cry. Not just any cry, but a boohoo-ugly cry. I think I may have asked the Lord to help me. I was on my knees, and probably even balled up, on the floor in front of the stove. I don't know if I was afraid of the fire because

I really couldn't focus on that. I was immediately afraid of me and my thoughts.

It was in that moment that I realized my mind was not clear. I had one too many thoughts going through my mind; one too many issues that I had hoped could be fixed (by singing, poetry, church, work, keeping people out of my personal space), and I had one too many issues that I believed were being fixed because I had faith and was a servant of God. That was the perception I had grown to believe. But also in that moment, I became real with God. And for the first time that I can truly remember, I was vulnerable with God. I was human for a change, and I cried out to Him while sitting on my kitchen floor. That Sunday I went to church and praised God really good. I danced for the first time in a long time, and I went on with my life.

And my life did go on, and I was fine for a while. Quite a bit of time would go by before I felt that way again—emptiness and heaviness at the same time. But even more time would pass before I would be able to actually identify a real issue. I can tell you, depression never *ever* was an apparent cause for the way I was feeling, but it makes so much more sense to me now. I wasn't crazy. I was *not* possessed by the devil. I simply was (and am) a young lady who did not know how to properly manage (negative) emotions and who was unaware of the effect mismanagement could have on my heart, on my life.

I can, however, conclude by saying that I have been back to Savannah quite a few times and taken a ride down White Bluff Road. The big tree is now simply that—a big tree.

Suppressing Depression

I HAD HAD my share of combat stress. Quite honestly, it was nothing compared to that of others who had endured the woes of war that were unfamiliar to me except through conversation, the news, and the Internet. So, for me, it seemed—and still sometimes seems—unfair to say that my time in Afghanistan was, or is, the *root* of my depression. Although I had not considered it, depression had been evident in my life well before I chartered a plane halfway around the world to support this not-so-agreeable war. I suppose it was only after I returned that I was able to identify it more easily.

I remember when I returned home. February 2010. At first, everything around me seemed to be okay. I managed to catch up on the sleep I had missed in the previous twelve months; I didn't have to go to work; my bills were minimal. Life was, in essence, good.

And then one day, out of nowhere, I was sad, and I had this uncanny feeling that I wanted to return to Afghanistan.

Life, I told myself, seemed so much better while deployed. I talked with a few of my soldier friends and learned they felt the same way. So, with that in mind, I dismissed my feelings, concluded they were normal, and attempted to move on. But that was so much easier to believe than it was to actually do.

The issue was this: no one at home cared. Or at least, no one seemed to care. Life at home had not stopped just because I was gone. So while I attempted to pick up where I left off a year prior, everyone else had new things going on. Granny was finally comfortable in her new house, which had been purchased before I left. My brother had a newborn son. My sister was now living states away. My mother was contemplating going back to school. Church was on a whole other plateau, with many new members, a lot of old ones gone, and was on the verge of relocation. Everything familiar to me was now unfamiliar, except God—but even He seemed rather distant and uninterested in my apparent dilemma.

Soon enough depression set in. However, I did not readily accept it for what it was. I only knew I felt extra sad. I was beginning to cry. (I had long since groomed myself to not cry.) I began to feel like I was behind in life and running out of time. I remember finding solace in planning my thirtieth birthday party. Eventually, that too would bring me grief.

I began to look for work, mainly because that's what I was supposed to do, but also because I thought being busy would help. I had grown accustomed to moving at a fast pace, and my position on my futon was prohibiting that. I needed to make moves. When an opportunity to assist my unit became available, I took it. It was not until later that I realized I shouldn't have. In all of this, I was still sad and began to seek an escape. From going back to school to relocating to another city, I had to *fix* myself.

As much as I tried to keep my feelings to myself, I couldn't. I was an expert when it came to hiding my emotions, but this time my skills were futile. Eventually, spending some time with myself would cause me to subconsciously cry out for help. (But let me inform you: there was nothing wrong with me.) I suppose I must have had a conversation with the unlikeliest of sources, my mother. The other particulars of the moment escape me now. I only know that I felt like I had no purpose and had begun to rehearse the all-I-would-ever-be speech.

Within days, my mother gave me a plant and a greeting card embossed with encouraging words. She encouraged me by reminding me that God had a plan for me, and that I mattered. She listed the title of a music album, along with a few of the song titles I had begun to work on years prior. She mentioned other aspects of the many plans and dreams I had discussed over the years. And I cried. (Looking at the card in this moment still brings tears to my eyes.) That would be encouragement to be strong and press on, at least for the moment. That was in April 2010.

Seeking the Source of My Pain

I would continue to suppress my feelings for quite some time. Because a few of these feelings seemed familiar to me, I knew I had to do something about it, or at least needed to talk about it. So I emailed my mom, and without disclosing the details of my latest epiphany, I asked her if she had ever dealt with depression. Although I knew not to readily expect a distinct answer, I was hoping she'd appease me this one time. And she did, albeit short and sweet. Any other response would not have been by my mother.

That email was sent to my mom many months after she had given me that encouraging card I mentioned earlier, and after that thirtieth birthday celebration I had so diligently anticipated. I had a job. I was back in school. I had even tried to date. Life was changing. *I* was changing. My heart still felt the same though—heavy and overwhelmed. I had sent that email because I wanted answers. I wanted to know *why* I felt this way. I wanted to know if anyone else (in my family) had struggled with depression.

Yes, I had finally diagnosed myself and was accepting this issue as my own, but it was something I could no longer deal with alone. I had been depressed before, but not quite like this. Before, I had learned to identify it, because it would happen around the same time every year—late September, early October—leading up to my birthday or during the days (sometimes months) following my birthday. Before I had learned to identify it, it was much more of a beast. But its beastly ways had calmed, my bouts surfaced less often, and I began to handle depression like a champ. After Afghanistan though, which I've referenced quite a bit already, depression had a new face: it looked like me.

I was dealing with emotions with which I had never dealt before. I had not felt these feelings before. I had more responsibilities and was dealing with an insurmountable level of stress. I was taking classes online, which was not as much of a breeze as I presumed it'd be. I had a job; I did not know earning a check could be so stressful. I was now a minister in church. I didn't feel ready, but I figured it would somehow bring me closer to God and cause me to at least redevelop my prayer life. I had tried to date; I readily established I wasn't relationship material and buried, once again, any desire for love and marriage. I felt displaced at church—no sense of belonging whatsoever. And I still wanted to relocate to another city. Persons I respected convinced me to stay a little while longer until. (All of the things that followed *until* have come to pass. I'm still in the same city, albeit reluctantly.)

It's funny because, even with all of these various emotions, I insisted I was "fine." And I was. There was nothing wrong with me. Fellow soldiers said I was angrier since the deployment. My grandmother said I was paranoid. But what do they know? One or two people from church offered prayer. And, eventually, I would have a meeting with my pastor (about something else). He would agree with my assistant who had, on more than one occasion, politely suggested I seek professional help. Finally making a pact with wisdom, I would go to speak with a counselor.

*Emotionally, I can say I've been somewhat,
no, I've been stable…
Mentally—I have my moments
but I still don't think
it's worth going to the head doctor for.*

—*9 Aug 2011*

Tell Me About Your Childhood

It was almost exactly two years since returning home from Afghanistan, and I was finally sitting in a counselor's office talking about my readjustment period and how life was going for me since coming home. I spent the bulk of the first session telling the counselor about how I really didn't need to be there because, again, there was nothing wrong with me. I told her how I was only there because my assistant had been pressing me about it for a year, and how my pastor agreed with that assistant when I told him about the suggestion. I told her how he had said that spiritual counseling was good, but it was okay to seek secular, or professional, counseling as well. I can respect him for choosing not to be my doctor.

She looked at me as if she wanted to laugh. I suppose she had seen my type before. You know, the type that insists they're "fine." The type that knows nothing's wrong with them. The type that only makes her way into the counselor's office because someone else suggested it. Look, I didn't really care what she was thinking. I didn't care to talk to her or anyone else. I simply needed her to agree that I was indeed fine, and that I really didn't need to be in her office.

Needless to say, an appointment was made for a second session.

Filled with a series of required questions that the counselor must ask of the "combat veteran," the first session was as grueling as expected. Nevertheless, I answered her questions honestly, but not without hopes that there were no signs of the unseen wound infamously known as post-traumatic stress disorder or PTSD. (Even with the dividends that could later be paid out to the suffering soldier, no one wants to deal with the disease. It only translates to crazy. No one wants to be called crazy—even if she is.) So I answered wisely but as honestly as possible.

Anyhow, the questions and the talking she allowed me to do were merely a setup. Seeing my reluctance to be there in the first place, the counselor was simply buffering me for the big whammy: tell me about your childhood. What? I did not come here for this! My childhood? What's that got to do with anything? Really, she had somehow listened to my responses about my deployment and life since, and managed to conjure up some unspoken hypothesis that my issues were not directly tied only to my deployment. Maybe there was something bigger, something deeper, and the deployment was simply the surface. For my counselor, learning about my childhood and predeployment life altogether was necessary for her investigation. She would get to the bottom of things even if I didn't want to.

I can't remember if it was session one or two—for pride's sake, let's say it was two—but I do know that by the end of it, I had shed a few tears. The type of tears that rush uncontrollably from the corners of the eyes, and no matter what a person does, she cannot stop them. Yeah, those tears. And it was in that moment that I found myself contemplating the death of (my) counseling. That woman had made me cry! Doesn't she know who I am? I. Don't. Cry. (At least not out loud or where other people can see me.) She had pried into my childhood, into my life, albeit innocently. She was concerned with the possibility of how long I had been experiencing certain emotions, and if they may have perhaps been present pre-Afghanistan.

If this had been a tug-of-war or something, I surely would have lost. (I simply would have gotten my revenge by not returning for another session.) But it was not a game. It was not a competition. If anything, it was an intervention (but it didn't stop my reluctance). The lady was destined to help me get to the bottom of things. Nothing more, nothing less.

Since I had dragged myself to the counseling center anyway, I may as well play along. Besides, I had shed tears. I don't have tears to waste.

Amber Alert

Considering the nature of the conversation, I realized that it was not me who cried but the girl inside of me who I thought no longer existed. My counselor—anyone who could dig so deep could no longer be the counselor—had managed to get water from a dry well. She had resuscitated the life of my inner child and caused her to want to live again.

There's only one thing about that: it was too late. That child was taken hostage years ago, and when I couldn't pay the ransom, she balled herself up and petitioned to be left alone. (I thought she had died.) But it was apparent that my counselor had a plan. By probing, I mean asking questions about my childhood, she indirectly issued an APB for me. I had to let myself go if I wanted to survive and live another day. I didn't know how I would do that, I wasn't convinced I could do that. I had long since learned how to suppress any emotions of care, concern, love—intimacy in any form—and living was no longer an option, but simply a chore I had been assigned, because God had not yet decided it was my time to die.

It is alarming that I would not make such an assessment until now; however, I can say it was the reality of the time. I had given up most on everything, on doing anything, or sharing my life with anyone. I had, more than once, lost complete interest in living, and eventually, it became a chore. The little girl was no longer intrigued, the grown woman was only interested in survival. Who needed all of the other stuff.

And this is what I wanted Ms. Counselor to understand: I was fine. I didn't need to be in her office. I didn't need to talk about my childhood. So yes, the war within me continued. There was no freeing of the trapped little girl within. *I did not come here for this!* But that little girl was now reaching through the bars, making an attempt to get a handful of freedom.

If for no other reason than for that little girl, I returned for the next scheduled session.

I'm still going to counseling…
I'm scheduled biweekly, which is good
because I was about to shut down
on her—the counselor—and not go back.
But I'm still going
& it seems to be doing a little bit of good.
I'm getting a little weary of talking about my childhood
but I suppose there's a point to it all.

—24 Mar 2012

Unlikely Medicine

WITH MY EMPHATIC reluctance, it would seem that I would give up on counseling rather quickly. But I didn't. (Well, I did, but I couldn't allow myself to not give it a real try.) It may also even surprise you to know that I am still attending regularly scheduled sessions, although I really hope to have a different testimony by the time you are reading this book. It has been a little over a year now since I made my way into the counseling center. I'd be lying if I said I have continued to fight every session because the truth is, I haven't. Now don't get me wrong. I do not always want to go. The thing I've learned is that I kind of have to go, if for no other reason than to talk to someone other than myself—and okay, God—about what I'm feeling. It's the one place I can go and trust that I won't be sent away in judgment and scribbled a prescription for prayer to assist me with my demons.

I can recall a few times when I was actually happy about going to a session. These times were when I was having a good or "healthy" week, and I was ready to expose the accomplishment in hopes of being freed from the punishment I had unwantedly received: counseling. I somehow made myself believe that if I could go into my counselor's office with a good report, she'd readily see I no longer needed her services, and she would send me on my way with progress notes worthy of framing. Much to my surprise, that's not exactly how it works.

And now I see why. My good and healthy reports in one session had been downgraded to reports of gloom by the next. There was no consistency in my emotions, and little did I know, I was on the roller-coaster ride of my life.

Only if You Swallow

It took me a minute to come to terms with the fact that I was really going someplace to talk to someone about my problems. Of course, to me there was nothing wrong, and I didn't need help. Other people said otherwise, but surely, I was not in the business of proving them right. Nevertheless, here I am. And I'm finally realizing that talking has been one of the most potent medications that have been prescribed to me. I use to hate to talk. Now every other week around 3:00 p.m., I go and expose the contents of the composition notebook confined to the corridors of my mind to someone who chooses to listen to me and others like me.

Here's what I have learned: medicine (and I'm specifically speaking of that taken orally) is only beneficial to you if you swallow it. Otherwise, if you have no intention of swallowing, it's pointless. Why put the meds in your mouth in the first place? (As a matter of fact, the only reason people put medicine in their mouths and don't swallow is because someone is watching, and they need to be deceptive.) I guess the point is not swallowing only hurts you.

One of the reasons I have been in counseling (so long) is because I walked into my counselor's office with my mind made up that I didn't need to be there. And I was pretty sure that every time would be my last time coming back. I had no intention of swallowing. I had diagnosed myself many times over as healthy and fine, and there was nothing she could tell me that I couldn't learn in my own home and through prayer. (Coincidentally, neither of these things proved to be effective at the time.) One day, when I requested to have fewer sessions (or none at all), my counselor let me know that I had been too (emotionally) inconsistent. I could not stop the sessions just yet. Ugh! It's been a year. But for most of that year, I had been reluctant to swallow.

Today my struggle is less intense, but for more reasons than one. I'm not so intimidated by the counseling process anymore. I still avoid the tell-me-about-your-childhood moments, no matter how relevant they may be to my healing—my *complete* healing. I still try not to cry, and if I do, I don't let the vulnerability during one session dictate if I will return for the next. I am no longer being forced to take my medication. Although the embarrassment of exposing myself always lingers, I cannot help but to acknowledge the changes that have taken place in my life through the most unlikely source. I had only considered the church. And although that is a good place to start, it may not be the place to end (at least not without a detour or two). I did not want to talk to a counselor—therapist, psychologist, social worker, whatever—and I did not want to be deemed crazy. (Truth is I probably would not have even sought mental help had my pastor not suggested it.)

I do not think I am crazy—naturally, I would think so. I also do not feel like something's wrong with me. I only know that I processed and dealt with things differently and internally, which caused me to carry the weight of my problems in an unhealthy way. Counseling (or therapy) is medicine. I have learned that it's not a sign of weakness if I go; it's only a façade of strength if I don't.

I have an appointment this afternoon.

> *Beloved, I wish above all things that thou mayest prosper and be in health, even as thy soul prospereth.*
> —3 John 1:2

*I'm drifting away again. Or at least beginning to.
I'm wanting to be left alone
and don't really want to do much.
I suppose depression is starting, or
trying to get started, up again.
But there won't be any of that.
Not this time.
So I'm trying to keep pushing socially,
emotionally, spiritually, holistically...*

—*24 March 2012*

Intermission
The Bright Side

It is a beautiful day here in Florida as I pen the beginning thoughts of this chapter. But who would have considered there would be such sunshine after a night like last night. The wind beat against my home as if it were seeking a place of refuge, while also sounding the alarm of the storm that was to come. The pores of the sky opened securely; thunder and lightning made their appearance. Together they, the winds, the rain, the thunder, the lightning, were in concert giving the city the darker side of nature's symphony: a storm. But there is no residue of any of that now. It looks the way Florida is supposed to look—like sunshine.

I cannot help but to be encouraged by such change, as it holds the appearance of everything good. The sunshine suggests that all things are well, and that the storm does not last forever. Oddly enough though, there is no assurance of that truth while in the middle of the storm. Everything is not good. (And frankly, I would like for people to stop saying everything is or will be all right in response to what is to me a dilemma.) I would like to believe God is with me, but if I can continue to be honest, I'd have to say that oftentimes I don't believe (or feel) that He is. I'm not going to say I don't believe He cares; I'll just say He's way too quiet sometimes.

"Weeping may stay for the night, but rejoicing comes in the morning" (Ps. 30:5, NIV).

I am not sure as to why God waits until the nighttime in life to get quiet. It kind of reminds me of the story of when Jesus was sleeping in the bottom of the ship during the storm, and the disciples were afraid and went down to get Him (see Mark 4:37–41). Oh, the dismay when they found Jesus asleep! How could Jesus have the nerve to sleep during the storm and let them die? The disciples were a bit upset, but Jesus would point out their downfall: there was a lack of faith.

I understand the disciples. The interesting thing, however, is that Jesus was with them the *whole time*. He may have been sleeping, but He was there. And that is something I have had to comprehend in my own life. God has a way of being absolutely silent during those times in which I feel I most need Him. I'm guilty of kicking and screaming every now and then, and needless to say, God does not move. But then there are those times when I make an adamant request. I disturb His rest. He commands peace to be still in my life, but then He lovingly reprimands me and questions the condition of my faith. Usually, I have no clear answer because I know that I have not been the most faith-filled person. Then I wonder why I don't trust God—He's brought sunshine before, He can do it again.

I suppose this is the place where I encourage myself, but as I consider the time and read through past journal entries, I realize that the bright side was simply a figment of my imagination (most of the time). I went in and out of the nostalgic motions hoping that someday I would no longer remember what it felt like to be loveless; to give but not receive, much less know *how* to receive; or to feel like the outsider in every group or in every room. I wanted to know what it felt like to belong, but I had long since accepted the fact, or at least the idea, that I never would.

Eventually, I was okay with it. Or I made myself be okay with it. If there was a bright side to any of the negativity I was given, I received, I harbored, I employed as defense, or any of the sort, then surely, I needed only be a little more patient and trust that my hope would not die. It would probably take way more time than it had already, but eventually, I would smile a genuine smile. I would laugh from my gut. I could dance without any music, or without anyone to help me keep the beat. I would love from my heart. I would live with all of my soul.

There is a bright side, and I had to learn to train myself to believe that the sun does shine after there has been rain. God will make sure of it.

Coming soon: 366 days to make God smile.
That's not me being deep
that's me keeping myself free from people and their woes.
After time, one grows weary of trying to make everybody happy,
inadvertently missing God
'cause for a minute "they" were god.
It's improbable I'll be free
as long as I keep placing people's needs before my own.
But such is my plight.
It's the way of this life—ministry.
I don't care to follow tradition but, if I must,
I resolve to evolve,
involve myself in my own happiness.
And the key to this hopeful bliss:
to take every day—all 366—and make... God... smile.

—2012 Resolve

Enough is Enough

There's nothing wrong with being tired.

—Bishop T. D. Jakes

AT SOME POINT, a choice must be made. Whether you want them to or not, your heart and mind somehow meet in agreement and, with (or without) your consent, they move forward in wanting better, living better and choose to drag you along for the ride. If it seems as if I'm talking psychologically and daring to split who you are into different parts, then you're right—I am. Sometimes we have to talk to ourselves. (Okay, so you really want me to believe I'm the only one who does it? Okay, that's fine.) At any rate, I am a witness that sometimes the heart doesn't do what the mind tells it to do, and oftentimes, we ignore any input from the spirit side of us. It can perhaps be likened to Paul's dilemma that we read about in Romans, chapter seven. He was a man wanting to do good—who knew how to do good—but when those times came, evil was present.

Depression is the extreme of sadness, hence the evil side of happiness (or "good").

Too Tired to Care

31 Dec 2012

> I don't really care to [spend] any time reflecting on the highs and lows of 2012. Truth is, the year's generally been low—all year. And I guess it can be summed up as a year of depression and a rollercoaster in my mind and emotions. (A ride I can only hope has come to an end.)

It was December 31st, and I was on the brink of another new year. And really all that means for me anyway was that it was time to go to yet another "watch night" service, a ritual slowly becoming less important to me than it once was. It was simply religion now and was only another service where I know my heart would be absent. I wrestled with whether or not I would stay home this New Year's Eve. And, naturally, my religion won. I went to church.

I was so tired though. At this point, I was sure I did not want to go to church anymore. 2012 had been that year, and in spite of my lofty resolution, I had given in, more than once, to the silent frustrations of my life and was running out of options. In 2012, I finally made my way into a counselor's office. I (reluctantly) talked about my childhood. That summer, I had my first real breakdown since that moment in my apartment on White Bluff Road roughly ten years prior. I cried more than I could remember up to that point. I was confused about what to do with church. (I was sure I didn't want to go anymore, or at least *just go* and do nothing else.) I was more than stressed at my job. I wanted to leave town. I wanted to run away. I was lonely. I was afraid. I was confused. I was tired. And here I was in church—again—making myself smile the smile, praise the Lord, play the part.

I was sure I had no energy for any of it. I had not thought about suicide or any other extreme measure; I was just going to leave. To go where, I don't know; but I wrestled so long already with the idea of relocating that, by this point, I just wanted to go somewhere where no one knew my name.

As I think about this time now, I realize that I was simply tired. The frustrating part about it is the fact that quite a few years had passed, and it seemed like I was falling into the same mind traps as I had done before. Why couldn't I learn the lesson? Why couldn't I better manage my emotions? I was a real adult now—I should know how to take better care of myself. Ugh! I remember one of the points my counselor continued to hone in about often was the fact that I needed to rest. Maybe it was time I took heed. Even more than taking my rest though, I needed to make up my mind that I would no longer allow myself to continuously go through this cycle.

29 April 2012

> I wish I could really pinpoint what is wrong with me, if anything at all. I've begun to not care about anything. It's a miracle that I get up and go to work or church every day…I guess I'm tired in my mind, in my soul. I don't know….My emotions are bankrupt but I somehow keep it moving, encouraging other people…By the time I'm 35, I'm sure I'll look back on these years and smile. For now, I just want things to be "normal." Though this seems to be "my" normal, it doesn't seem to work for me anymore.

It was time to *choose* something different, something new. I had wandered in the wilderness of my emotions long enough—it was time to cross over into the Promised Land. But I didn't know how I would do that. I had been in counseling for months, and talking about it, to me, just didn't seem worth it. But that didn't matter. I would use my resources. And eventually, I would pray and not be concerned about God not hearing me.

The Call

The details of the evening are more of a blur than I care for them to be—well, maybe not—but I know I was trying to enjoy the New Year's Eve service without putting in any extra work. I sat somewhere in the back, my usual spot, and I tried not to look like I did not want to be there. I surprisingly endured the service, choosing not to overreact with emphatic amens and other gestures to cheer on whoever might have the microphone at the moment (or to appear that I felt any spirit). Eventually, all events for the evening would be complete, the sermon was preached, and it was time for the invitation to accept Christ as Savior. At some point between the end of the sermon, the call to salvation, and the benediction, another invitation was made. Most of the people were dancing, singing, shouting—praising God—and getting excited about whatever declaration they had just made that would ensure the coming year would be nothing like the last. I was not moved.

I guess, like I have said already, I just wasn't interested. I wasn't interested in being there. I wasn't interested in repeating a lot of catchphrases, especially if it only meant receiving it for the moment. I wasn't interested in an emotional ending to 2012 or beginning of 2013. If I was going to allow anything to happen to me in that service, it would need to be genuine.

And that moment eventually came when the pastor started praying for certain conditions, ailments, and the like. I was as into the moment as I possibly could be while I made observations, ensuring I, or anyone else, didn't get knocked over, trampled upon, or hit. So the pastor would call out a need and challenge the people who had that need to respond in a particular way. He eventually asked for anyone who had dealt with depression during that year to run up here and dance. Now *up here* meant where he was. He was in the front of the church; I was in the back. *Dilemma*. But I challenged myself long enough, but not too long to miss the blessing of the moment. I ran to the front. I danced. I cried. I danced. I chose to not walk out of that service without giving God at least one more chance to help me live free of depression. I couldn't focus on whether or not it would work this time, or how long my joy or happiness would last. I had danced in front of the church and in that moment, I had ousted myself as a depressed Christian. This had better worked.

Freedom of Choice

I must remember that God's silence is not His neglect; on the contrary, it is simply His forbearance of my inability to trust Him while He listens to me relish in my apparent internal agony. He waits on me to finish and, like in the case of Job, answers me after I've demanded answers, and He is sure He can't take any more of my ranting. But I can appreciate that. I can appreciate the fact that God does not impose His will on us, upon me. *The beauty of free will.* But then I suppose there's also its danger—I could very well choose to die. Death, however, could no longer have rank on my list of resorts. I had to decide to live and live well.

And that was the new, conscious conclusion: I would live. I had no other choice. Not this time around. Perhaps there was a repressed fear that this time there was no turning back (if death had been my tentative resolve). And no matter how much it crossed my mind in the past, I knew I was not ready to die. Oddly enough, I was not afraid of dying, I was just certain I was not quite ready to go just yet. Nonfear of death aside, I had to live. And it was not enough to live for everyone else—that hadn't gotten me too far anyway. I had to live for me. I didn't know how I was going to stay on the right track *this time*, but I was determined to live and not die. I was determined to smile more than I frowned, laugh more than I cried. I was determined to allow myself to happen to life rather than always surrendering to it happening to me. It was time I put my foot down and not pick it up. I had to make a statement, take a stand. Reclaim my emotions, reclaim my mind, reclaim my life. Because I was tired, I figured it must be time to do something different. Walking away from church seemed to be a good idea at the time. Shutting down again on family and friends didn't seem to be as much of a formidable idea as it once was—I knew it'd not have much effect. I wanted to rid myself of the redundancy of religion, Christianity or otherwise. Enough was enough. And this time I was sure.

*I chose sadness today
for fear that happiness would return
only to leave again.
That is a burden I can no longer bear.*

—*4 April 2013*

D-DAY

IN A PARTICULAR week, about three or four days had passed me by in a blur, and it was as if they had never come. All I remember is that I stayed in my bed under the covers, blinds closed, getting up only to do what was necessary; leaving the house for appointments that I only chose to keep to save face and demean the appearance that something was wrong. The emotions that prescribed my bed rest are all a blur—they were a blur at that time as well—and therefore I have no true explanation as to why I was overcome, or perhaps had given in, to depression once again.

It had been about three or four months since deciding enough was enough, denouncing the spirit of depression—or more lightly put, emotional instability—and all the other issues that came with it, like fear and anxiety. I was doing well. I had repented to my pastor for being unavailable for ministry because repentance shows I'm absolutely ready to make a change, right? And I was making a deliberate effort in every other area in my life to just do better. I got out of the bed every day. I cleaned up my home. I began to open the blinds every day. I began submitting school assignments on time. I made myself available.

I went to my counseling sessions with slight joy, anticipating the diagnosis that would free me from what was now routine care. But I wouldn't get my freedom papers. I, to her, was somewhat inconsistent, unstable in my emotions. She said there was some anxiety, a little PTSD. She said it was a mild stage. Huh? But I'm fine! I've yet to see her notes about this, but I had long since learned to trust my counselor, and as frustrated as I wanted to be, I took the time to consider her words.

Maybe she was right.

Meanwhile

I cannot remember how or why, but I would have a setback. Maybe it was because of the man with whom I was trying to make a relationship work. Maybe it was my job situation. Perhaps it was my familial relationships. I don't know (although I could probably figure it out if I took the time to read a few journal entries). Anyhow, whatever it was, it had led me to the place in which I began this chapter: in the bed. I had cried a few times. For what, who knows? I wasn't working. I was out of money. I was feeling pretty neglected.

I wanted a new beginning, a new start and had no clue as to how to go about making the proper moves to get this new start. I was at the end of completing the final courses for my graduate degree. I had plenty to smile about. Or at least I thought I did. But I was so unsure about life. Seemingly, I was at a dead end—again—and was about to accomplish new things, but have nothing to really show for them.

In the midst of my pity party—because in essence and in retrospect, that is perhaps all it really was—I took a moment to see what else might be going on in the world. I flipped the channels. I perused a favored social media site. Wait. Stop. Go back. What happened? The son of a prominent pastor had committed suicide. I began to cry. I began to pray. I had no choice but to offer praise. Not because a father and mother no longer had their son, but because my father and mother still had their daughter. I realized that that weekend's headline could have very well been my own. I prayed for the family and cried for my brother who was no longer here. I cried longer than I can remember. With every tear came another ounce of gratefulness, another jolt of strength. I eventually got up out of the bed. I eventually made my bed, opened the blinds, combed my hair, and everything else. The next morning I prepared for Sunday service in a solemn fashion. Brother Warren was on my mind, and so was the heaviness of the hurting, heavy soul of the many others like him, like me, who suffer with themselves and go to battle with themselves by themselves more often than they should. I would pray for that population of people who had decided they had done all they could do and were contemplating ways out.

Sunday Morning

I will not forget that Sunday morning. It was the epitome of the bright side. My heart was filled with both sorrow and praise. Sorrow because the news still weighed heavy on my heart, and also because of the probability that there were many other people, particularly Christians, who were suffering with and or within themselves. I could only imagine the number of people who might have spent the week in the bed like I did but who did not make it to see the week's end. The possibility frightened me.

My heart was filled with praise because I was still alive and able to praise the Lord for keeping me alive. He had kept my mind when I no longer really cared for its keeping. And for the first time in a while, I was in church that morning because I wanted to be. I didn't have to drag myself there that day in order to find my life; rather, I chose to go because I had my life.

The words of the song being sang by the praise team that morning became my unapologetic refrain: "the devil tried to defeat us, but we come out victorious!" It was time for me to take my place at the podium to read the scripture for the day. I was not taking a place at the podium to sing, but I could not let go of the song. With Brother Warren, with my own life, and often-battled mind on my mind, I sang the words and grabbed hold of my own victory with every repeated note. I was a child of God. I was a healed child of God. I was a victorious child of God. I was going to live *now*, and there was not anything that even I could do about it.

That first Sunday in April was a day of deliverance. It was my D-day. Has everyday been easy since then? Absolutely not. Have I cried since then? Absolutely—and much more than I remember. But what I can assure you of is this: I am *healed*. Depression may attempt to set in from time to time, but I remember how victory felt that day, and I do what I must to try to remain victorious. Some days are harder than others. Some nights are much longer than others. But then there's God. Then there's me. And with His help, I experience D-day all over again. There's nothing like it.

The Lord is my strength and my shield; my heart trusted in him, and I am helped: therefore my heart greatly rejoiceth; and with my song will I praise him.

—Psalm 28:7

The joy of the Lord is your strength.

—Nehemiah 8:10

The Lord is my shepherd, I lack nothing.
He makes me to lie down in green pastures,
he leads me beside quiet waters,
he refreshes my soul…

—Psalm 23:1–3, NIV

Thou hast turned for me
my mourning into dancing:
thou hast put off my sackcloth,
and girded me with gladness;
To the end that my glory may sing praise to thee,
and not be silent.
O Lord my God,
I will give thanks unto thee for ever.

—Psalm 30:11–12

All Is Well

But thou, O Lord, art a shield for me;
my glory, and the lifter up of mine head.

—Psalm 3:3

There is not too much more I can say at this point. Or maybe there is not much more I need to say about me and my struggle. I would love to emphatically declare that the struggle is over, but that would not be my truth. I can say, however, that all things are well. Do I always feel well? Do things always look well? Probably not. Nevertheless, I have faith in the victory that I have obtained through Jesus Christ. Like Paul, I can say I have learned to do with and without, and in all things to be content. Because of the sustainability of Christ, I am able to stand and do all things.

I pen this chapter with a smile. Not because everything is lovely as a bed of roses in this moment, but there is the acceptance of the mere possibility that someday there will be the bed of roses, and none of them will die (at least not as quickly as usual). I have realized the power of making decisions, and making them for myself. I have come to understand that God really does do all things well, even when or if I cannot comprehend the things He does. I have learned that it is okay to be sad. It is okay to cry. It is okay to have a bad day. It is okay to express myself in the moment. If I am happy, I can be happy. But if I am not too happy, I have learned that it is okay to tell the truth. I should've paid attention to Jesus earlier when He said, "The truth shall make you free" (John 8:32). So often, I have believed that He was talking about the Word of God, but now I am sure that He was simply talking about the *truth*. The truth in all matters—in life, in love, in situations, and in circumstances. A person must be truthful about what is going on in her life if she is to live and be free. Man, that Jesus really was on to something.

A New Normal

Some days are so much better than others. I have even had a few days where I struggled to maintain the victory in my emotions. Even still, it's not a struggle every day; it's not a battle every day. And I smile because I realize I do have joy every day even if and when the happiness seems to be nonexistent. Even more than that, I have peace in my mind and in my life. I get frustrated from time to time because I am still learning the ins and outs of this *new me*, but I have not thought to drop out of class. Sure, I miss the old me probably too often, but I don't miss the days when I couldn't comprehend what was going on inside of me, inside of my mind. I thank God for understanding.

The hard reality is that depression is a weighty spirit, and if I am not careful, it will find a way to bombard my life and take residence once again. So I focus more on God. That is a part of the secret to my success, if there is any. He will keep me in perfect peace if I keep my mind on Him. And as selfish as this could sound, I focus on myself more. Making other people happy is great; however, when you find yourself empty, more often than not, it is time to do inventory. And that's what I had to do for my emotions. I knew how to do it in other areas of my life, but for some reason, I thought considering myself was simply selfish in nature, so I often denied—and sometimes I still deny—myself for the sake of others. Loving others and putting their needs before my own is fine, but what good am I if I never consider myself?

So this is my *new normal*. This is why I can say all is well (even when I don't always feel it is). I have peace in my mind. I look in the mirror now and see the me I should see—the me God sees. I honestly see a glow about me every morning. Now it took some time for this. It didn't happen when I decided enough was enough or on D-day, but it eventually happened, and quite unexpectedly. But I smile now—just because. I talk more to people. And although it is sometimes a challenge, I express my feelings more. I still struggle in the love department—romantically, loving out loud and unafraid—and I still have an issue with the impact of words. (I just honestly believe they hold that much weight.) But I believe in myself now. I trust my opinion of myself more than other people's opinions of me. I smile now. I love now. I live now. *Now!*

The greatest war I'll ever fight is the war against the self. It definitely tops Afghanistan. It makes any struggle at school, on that school bus, in the church, or in my home look like a mere puppy love spat between two kindergarteners in the sandbox. But today, I can say that all is well because probably for the first time ever, I honestly believe my good days garner much more weight than the bad. My emotions are no longer on the roller coaster, which had, until now, seemingly become a very accommodating ride, albeit tiresome. And I have peace. I feel peace, and I can assure you there's not anything like it. I cry still, but I recover as quickly as possible. I no longer ignore the issues. I allow myself to feel, and I don't rush the process. Sure, that seems a little weird and quite contrary to the teachings of faith I have received for so long. But ignoring how I feel is much like sweeping dirt under a rug. Eventually, it will appear through the rug, and what was once used as a decorative floor covering becomes dusty, dirty, and tainted because the person never took the time to properly clean the floor. I now properly clean. If someone comes into my life when I just happen to need to do some cleaning, they'll have to choose to leave or accept me with my issues. I will not brush anything—any emotion, any hurt, any pain—under the rug in my life for the sake of saving face and appearing to have it all together. Not again.

I am in my personal campaign of boycotting fear. First item on the agenda: live. Christ has made all things new—emotionally, mentally, spiritually. He has made me glad. Everything and all is well. I embrace my struggle. I own it now, unafraid. I now know how to better cope, and when I feel I want to give up, I take a time-out and muster the audacity to ask God for strength and grace to go one more day. I refuse to die here. And I refuse to die depressed. Living is my plight. I gladly accept it.

> *I shall not die, but live, and declare*
> *the works of the Lord.*
>
> —Psalm 118:17

*I can't even remember what the dream was about.
I just know I woke up laughing.*

Part II

YOUR VICTORY

When God, for whatever reason, has wounded you,
you learn how to minister to others
with the same wound.

—Rabbi David Wolpe

And he said unto me, My grace is sufficient for thee:
for my strength is made perfect in weakness.
Most gladly therefore will I rather glory in my infirmities,
that the power of Christ may rest upon me.

—2 Corinthians 12:9

Prelude to Victory

Revelation 12:11 says, "And they overcame him by the blood of the Lamb, and by the word of their testimony…" For the purpose of this book, or at least this chapter, it is proper to specifically focus on the part, "the word of their testimony." This book is my testimony by which, in conjunction with the blood of the Lamb, I hope to overcome. But I don't want to cross over alone; I want to bring you with me.

As you have had opportunity to see into my life, better yet, my mind, I trust that you have already taken something from the words you have read. If not, then I challenge you to read on further. This section is for you. From where I am writing these words to where you are reading them, I join forces with you so that we together may combat the illness known as depression and all the extra things that come with it. I trust that as you continue to read, you will gain the strength you need to get out of bed another day, open the blinds another day, smile another day, laugh out loud another day, fight another day—*live* another day. We don't fight against flesh and blood, but rather principalities and powers—things outside our control that are simply a part of the enemy's arsenal, which by the way, is filled with no new tricks, to cause us to believe that we have to live a defeated life. But let it be known: God has given us the victory! Because of the work of the Cross, the enemy is already defeated, and we have already overcome. Let's fight together. Let's continue living together and do so victoriously. You're a winner—now.

A Fixed Fight

Just as determined as you are to live a full, undefeated, prosperous life in or outside of Christ, so then is your enemy. Everyone or everything has a purpose. The enemy of your soul, whether or not you proclaim to be a Christian, is purpose-driven. He is out to destroy you. Kill you. And he will do that by any means necessary (especially if you have chosen Christ over him). But even though the opposition seems to be so bent on fulfilling his purpose, there is hope. As determined as he is, so you have to be as well. After all, it is a fixed fight. Consider the following:

> Then upon Jahaziel the son Zechariah, the son of Benaiah, the son of Jeiel, the son of Mattaniah,

a Levite of the sons of Asaph, came the Spirit of the Lord in the midst of the congregation; And he said, Hearken ye, all Judah, and ye inhabitants of Jerusalem, and thou king Jehoshaphat, Thus saith the Lord unto you, Be not afraid nor dismayed by reason of this great multitude; for the battle is not yours, but God's. To morrow go ye down against them: behold, they come up by the cliff of Ziz; and ye shall find them at the end of the brook, before the wilderness of Jeruel. Ye shall not need to fight in this battle: set yourselves, stand ye still, and see the salvation of the Lord with you, O Judah and Jerusalem: fear not, nor be dismayed; to morrow go out against them: for the Lord will be with you. (2 Chron. 20:14–17)

The victory belongs to the believer. If you believe you can be healed, then you can. If you believe you can be set free, then you can. If you believe you can be whole, then *you can*!

I know it is easier for me to write this than it is to do it. I'm sure it is easier for you to read this than it may be for you to do it, but I'm a witness that it is doable. (It's the only way I'm even able to write this book.) You reach this place within yourself where you're so tired you don't even trust God is trying to listen to you anymore. But He's listening.

He is the only alternative for healing because He is the Absolute Healer, meaning, He can heal you from anything, even those things you don't talk about. He sees the sickness of the heart and mind, and He stands ready to deliver you out of the hand of the enemy. The spirit of the tormentor is trespassing in your life. You have complete authority to evict him. You've made it through half of the book. I trust you'll continue reading and gain the strength to reclaim your victory and thereby reclaim your life.

> *For God hath not given us the spirit of fear; but of power, and of love, and of a sound mind.*
>
> —2 Timothy 1:7

Hi, How Are You

*The only thing more tragic
than the tragedy that happens to us
is the way we handle it.*

—John Eldridge, *Wild at Heart*

No, seriously, how are you? For many years, whenever someone would ask me about my well-being, I would simply respond by saying fine. It was the way I had been taught to respond in spite of how I was really feeling at the time. I have since learned to say I'm okay or I'll be okay or I'm making it or anything that could be more close to the truth than fine. After all, most of the time, fine was a lie.

How many times have you chosen to resort to the simpler response in order to rid yourself of the inquirer, or to refrain from getting into the details of your personal life? That was usually my aim, and I had convinced myself that a simple "fine" was a surefire way to end the conversation.

Do people really care anyway? Do they just ask about how you're doing in order to be cordial enough so that they may politely trek their way to the probable selfish reasons for which they have approached you in the first place? For once, wouldn't it be nice to have someone to honestly ask about your well-being and stay long enough to hear your response in its entirety?

Maybe you are just fine today, blessed by the best, blessed and highly favored, too blessed to be stressed. I'm sure the list of proper responses for the church person goes on and on. (Quite frankly, half of the things we say are usually not our personal truths; they simply just feel good to say and sound good to hear.) At any rate, I would like to challenge you to give an honest answer. And there is no need to offer up a thesis statement or anything like that. But how much more could it hurt if you were to admit you're having a bad day or that you're doing okay, but you could sure use some prayer? Or maybe actually admit that you're feeling a bit under the weather—yes, we have a hard time with that too. God forbid people learn we do not really have any superpowers and we actually are human.

I guess the gist is to encourage honesty. Be true to yourself, be true to other people. I have come to learn that trying to smile instead of frown, or laugh instead of cry, or say "I'm fine" instead of "I'm hurting," takes a lot more energy than it seems, and eventually it catches up with a person.

Eventually, you have to tell the truth. And this is not to combat against the passage of scripture that encourages believers to speak a thing, and they shall have what they say (see Mark 11:23), or that life and death is in the power of the tongue (see Proverbs 18:21). Both of these texts are truth. Speaking positively is also a method encouraged in counseling, secular and Christian, so I'm not telling you to simply ignore hope and become a certified pessimist. Nevertheless, the Scripture does not neglect this: you shall know the truth and the truth shall make you free (see John 8:32).

The chapters that follow are included to simply help you find your way to, and declare, your own truth. If you are to be truly free, you must be able to identify the things that hold you bound. You must assess where you are. You must know where you are trying to go. And the truth will help you get there. By the end of your reading, I hope that your truth will be like mine: a declaration of victory and freedom. When someone asks how you are doing, you will be able to tell them and do so unashamedly. So, I ask again, how are you? Hopefully, by the end of this chapter—or maybe I'll give you till the end of this book—you will find yourself able to answer this question truthfully, honestly, with no holds barred.

*"Mental illness" is a poor term sounding like,
"It's just your mind."
But a broken brain is as physical as a broken bone.*

—Pastor Rick Warren

THE SILENT SUFFERER

THE WEIRD THING about depression is it gives the sufferer—you—the uncanny ability to function in the presence of others. Functional dysfunction. You know that functional ability that allows you to smile when you want to frown, laugh when you want to cry. It is when you're alone at home or in your car that you pick up where you left off, cue the music, and dance with the one thing that you'd much rather live without: depression. Sadly enough, your mental illness (in whatever form it comes) is seemingly the only consistent thing in your life. Sometimes, actually more often than not, it seems more consistent and more real than God. And it is in that moment of thought that the battle heightens and the wage of war is the life of the person who has been mentally raped of his will to live.

So what's a girl (or guy) to do?

I wish there was an easy answer to that question. I am a witness that when it comes to chronic sadness, depression, or mental illnesses and disorders, nothing's easy.

Declarations are as hard to say as they are to do, and choosing to believe that life and death is in the power of the tongue becomes a task so foreign, you feel like a toddler who is learning to walk or talk—it is almost too easy to crawl, to be carried, and cry and scream for what you want. I mean, let's face it: like a baby, you feel helpless, unable to save yourself, so you wait for someone—a parent, a spouse, a friend, a pastor, a doctor—to rid you of your inability and soothe your longing to smile and laugh again; to walk and talk again on your own.

You're Not Alone

"In my distress I cried unto the Lord, and he heard me" (Ps. 120:1).

Only God knows your pain greater than you do. And so no one else will suspect your silent struggle, you smile in the face of most everyone else. But as made evident at several points in this book, you are not alone. You are not the only one who has wrestled with herself or himself. Jacob, in Genesis 32, seemingly alone, realized he was not alone, as he wrestled with a man and refused to let him go without receiving a blessing. Take David also, a man whom God described as a man after His heart. He understood in whom was his help—his help simply came from the Lord (see Psalm 121:2). Maybe you feel like Jacob, and you wrestle all night unable to rest; or like David in the cave after he sought to save his life; or perhaps, like Elijah when he fled into the wilderness and sat under the juniper tree. Let's take it a step, a man, a prophet, further. Maybe you feel like Jesus when He went into the Garden of Gethsemane with an exceedingly sorrowful soul and asked God to take the cup away from Him. From the least to the greatest, from the sinner to the saint, from the believer to the nonbeliever, this one thing remains true: "We have not an high priest which cannot be touched with the feeling of our infirmities" (Heb. 4:15). Jacob was a man. Moses was a man. David was a man. Elijah was a man. *Jesus was a man.* And each of these men reached points in their lives when they felt as if they couldn't go on living with their burdens any longer.

If you read about Elijah's episode in 1 Kings 19, you will see that his stint underneath the juniper tree was actually a suicide attempt. Elijah literally asked God to take his life and said, "It is enough" (v. 4). He, in essence, had himself a pity party. He was depressed. Nevertheless, one thing is for sure: he was tired and felt he could not take it anymore—anymore of life's pressures, anymore of the burden of being a prophet, anymore of the ministry, anymore of the threats against his life. He felt just like you may feel sometimes. I know I share his sentiments. But God sent comfort to Elijah in the middle of his depression, when he had fallen asleep (and we all know that is when the pity party and depression has reached its climax). Elijah may have been done, but God was not done with Elijah. Jacob, David, and Jesus were also done, but God was not done with them—there was more work for them to do. And just like God sent comfort to the mournful souls of our predecessors, He can send comfort to you, us, and give you new joy. He can give you peace. He can restore your soul. Suffer if you must, and silently if you have to. But you, my friend, are not alone in this struggle.

A SILENT EPIDEMIC

We live in an age of melancholy.
Depression has replaced anxiety
as "the common cold of emotional life."

—John Ortberg,
The Life You've Always Wanted

TODAY, I STILL harbor deep thoughts about the news of a brother in Christ who, a couple of days ago, took his own life. I have never met the young man, but I am sure of the connection because otherwise, sorrow could not be so overwhelming.

It was news that shook me to the core as I read of the suicide of the son of Pastor Rick Warren, pastor of the Saddleback Church in Saddleback Valley, CA, and author of *The Purpose Driven Church* (1995) and *The Purpose Driven Life* (1997). Now I don't include this biographical snippet to give you any ideas other than good about Pastor Warren, rather, only to paint the background to a picture that often goes unseen.

Many people may have immediately begun to judge and question how the son of this pastor could take his own life. I, for one, immediately identified with him and began to cry. I realized that at some point in time that could have very well been me. When news surfaces about other Christians who decided they could no longer handle the pressures of life, the questions ensue, with people wondering how it could be possible that the persons were unable to be *saved*. Just because we know the secret anecdotes for living—God will keep him in perfect peace whose mind is stayed on him, or just pray and have faith, or take your burdens to the Lord and He will carry them—does not mean we always have the faith to believe those anecdotes or the strength to employ them. Sometimes, life is just that heavy. We have no clue what to do with it no matter how much, in our hearts, we want to trust God.

But that is a harsh reality to accept, especially for nonbelievers or those persons outside looking in. It is almost too easy for people to believe that because they never see you cry or frown or ask for help, you must not need anything. And because they see you in church working, praying—functioning—they remain oblivious to the possibility that life may very well be happening to you in a very distinct way, and you may have already decided that this service, this prayer, this cry will be your last. You silently suffer and fall prey to the disease that has silently crept into your life and chosen to eat away at the very core of who you are. It won't be satisfied until it steals your life.

Purpose-Driven Opposition

If you've made it to this point in the book, you already know why I connect so strongly with Brother Warren, as I feel he should affectionately be so called. You know my cause. When I started writing this book, I had only a minimal understanding of why I had to write it. Honestly, the idea came out of the blue, but I knew I had to write. And now my brother has confirmed the cause: Christians—"saved" ones, tongue-speaking ones, demon-casting-out ones, preaching ones, praying ones, loud ones, quiet ones—suffer. They suffer from the expected persecution that Jesus spoke of in Matthew 5:11–12. They suffer from, and with, temptation of sin. They suffer with pain, heartache, and loneliness. They suffer from sicknesses, seen and unseen, diagnosed and undiagnosed. Christians suffer.

I do not mind being the bearer of bad news here because it has been the undisclosed truth long enough. Think about it: how many believers give their lives to Christ but attempt to retake that life at the first sight of suffering? Some church, some pastor somewhere withheld the whole truth. Contrary to the popular consensus, choosing the Christian path does not negate human life. Nobody, Christian or not, is exempt from human suffering.

Sadly though, this is a hard pill to swallow. And rather than seek help for the unseen diseases, we deal with them in the privacy of our homes and tuck them away in the blacked out corridors of our hearts and minds until the point at which loneliness and sadness turns into anxiety and depression, and then depression into torment. It's a silent epidemic to outsiders, but inwardly, there is a screeching sound so intense that it tears at the soul like fingernails against the blackboard. At that point, only God dares pay attention. Sadly, also at that point, out of shame, distrust, and perhaps, many other emotions, you no longer have the strength to call God's name or reach for His hand. You lose your grip. You slip. You fall. You think you want to die, but the inaudible truth is you hope someone saves you.

That is the goal of depression and all of the emotions tied to it. The ones that carry it into your life—the boyfriend who broke your heart, the parent who abandoned you, the uncle who raped you, the friends who betrayed you, the parents who forsook you, the job you lost, the baby you abandoned, the church that disowned you—that come with sadness and loneliness, wearing them proudly on the sleeve because these are the things you can handle (or at least so you think). But depression is in the back pocket, tucked safely out of sight so that when you lose control and get so sad and so lonely that you feel your only companion is you—God's not even interested—it will overtake you gently. It's as if someone quietly places a pillow over your face while you're sleeping and in the middle of a pleasant dream, and you find yourself awakened, gasping for air. Depression has come to kill.

> The thief cometh not, but for to steal, and to kill, and to destroy: I am come that they might have life, and that they might have it more abundantly.
>
> —John 10:10

In a League of Its Own

Now perhaps, it is a farfetched assertion to say depression is in a league of its own, but for me, it is not so farfetched. Depression, as common as it may be, is still somehow in a class all by itself because it is not an illness that is as evident as others. A wound to the skin—a cut, a bruise, burns—is so much easier for a person to deal with, and my guess is it's because these wounds are visible to other people. And then there are some other illnesses that cause people to seek medical attention—some minor, like a cold, many others major, like cancer. And then there's depression. Maybe there is a stigma attached to depression that no one wants to have attached to themselves. Like I said in one of the earlier chapters, I did not want to be seen as crazy or unstable. In the army and in the faith-based world, I would have been told to suck it up and drive on (in the army) or take it to the Lord in prayer (in the church). Because of how mental illness is viewed by outsiders, the individuals dealing with these problems have the tendency to insist upon struggling with the problems by themselves. As a matter of fact, the National Institute of Mental Health asserts that "many people with a depressive illness never seek treatment."[1] It is apparent no one person wants to voluntarily become the eleventh member of the lepers. I don't blame him. Who wants to live life as an outcast? After all, isn't it so much easier to blend in with the crowd during the day and suffer silently—and alone—through the night in hopes that Jesus will soon pass by?

Coming in many forms, ranging from major depression to bipolar disorder, depression can last a few weeks or even years.[2] It affects a person's mood and his functionality. In this moment, I'm reminded of the hymn "Nobody Knows the Trouble I've Seen." It's a hymn that talks about being up sometimes and down sometimes. (Either way, not stable.) Talk about a Sunday morning pick-me-up. No wonder people are refusing to truly seek help in church. Everyone is depressed, or at least they should be, after singing such an anthem that only ministers to the hurt, amplifies the issues, and perhaps prescribes justification for a person to remain the way he is with nobody but Jesus at his side. And to think, "Glory hallelujah!" is included in that hymn. I'm not so sure there is anything glorious at all.

I digress, as it is not my desire to offer a critique on this beloved song. I simply use it to help paint a picture. If any person is to overcome depression (in a faith-based world), he or she must understand that Jesus does see the troubles, and other people have also experienced those same troubles. God sees, and He knows. He has given us each other in order to lean on each other, glean from each other, and overcome by the blood of the Lamb and the word of our testimony.

Even with that in mind, we must not be afraid to seek help. My pastor often says that God can heal by way of miracle or medicine. And one of the best pieces of advice he could give me out of all the sermons I heard him preach includes him telling me that it was okay to seek professional counseling. I may not have ever hauled myself into the counseling center that day over two years ago had he not agreed with other people in my life and made such a suggestion. (And I'd certainly not still keep my appointments two years later.)

Depression takes away your thrill for life. You no longer find joy in what you once enjoyed. Getting out of bed becomes a chore. And let's not talk about opening the blinds, or making it out of the house, or keeping a straight face at work, or hoping you can make it through the session without crying. Because, after all, nothing's wrong with you, right? Or maybe, like me, church has been your foundation and has been the center of your life, so for you it's not a matter of keeping a straight face. You have to smile at those people at church. They mustn't sense that something's wrong, and that you have somehow lost the faith. Of course, they usually never ask, but they will be apt to send you away with a farewell that sounds a little something like, "I'll be praying for you." Oddly enough, they never actually do anything. But you have to still sing that song as a member of the worship team or the choir, you have to usher, you have to film the services. (I wonder how many times someone has asked the cameraman if everything's okay with him. Truth is we probably never notice until there's no cameraman. Sad idea, isn't it?)

But just like that, depression eats away at the soul of a person, populating like maggots on his emotions until he erodes, eventually taking it out on himself or others or both. I thought of suicide. I was sure I didn't want to take anyone with me; somehow I feel that would have defeated my purpose. But it is obvious I was not quite ready to go either. For some other people, peace has not been so gracious. They have lost their lives or have hoped to lose it.

They have shut down on their friends and loved ones. They are just going through the motions, trusting someday it will get better. At some point, they stop wondering, *Why me?* And they choose to give up. I don't want you to be a part of those statistics.

Equal Opportunity Illness

Now that I have committed to writing this book, it seems strange to me that Christians, believers, the church—the faith-based world—would somehow rule out depression as an issue with which Christians would suffer. If I had a dime for every time I was told that whatever I was feeling was nothing but the devil, or that I needed to seek God for peace, or go on a fast and pray, I'm sure I'd be well on my way to taking that hopeful trip to Aspen or Tahiti. Taking my problems to the altar and leaving them there sounds easy enough; however, I'm sure if more of us would be honest, we'd learn that some of us are quite guilty of picking up those burdens while rising from our knees.

> And as Jesus passed by, he saw a man which was blind from his birth. And his disciples asked him, saying, Master, who did sin, this man, or his parents, that he was born blind? Jesus answered, Neither hath this man sinned, nor his parents: but that the

works of God should be made manifest in him. (John 9:1–3)

In the passage above, the disciples did not even consider an alternative for the blind man. They immediately questioned Jesus and inquired about who sinned. They were naturally convinced that someone, either the blind man or maybe his parents, had to have sinned, or else the man would not be blind. Jesus, however, saw an opportunity for the glory of God to be revealed. Even more wisely, Jesus contended that no one had sinned. Contrary to what many people, believers, may think, depression is not a "worldly" disease. It does not attach itself to a person as a result of sin. It does not care which god a man believes in or which one he chooses to worship. As suggested earlier in this chapter, choosing to become a Christian does not negate human life. And human life is not devoid of pain and suffering. And pain and suffering is not limited to a certain age, gender, race, or belief system of a people.

For 2013, the Center for Disease Control and Prevention (CDC) documents suicide among the top ten leading causes of injury deaths for persons ages ten and up.[3] Sadly, children in the 10–14 age group account for over three hundred out of the more than forty thousand suicide deaths in 2013, which includes suicide by firearm, suffocation, and poisoning.[4] And the numbers are even more startling with older groups, as they range in the thousands. This is alarming, to say the least.

Additionally, this broad age range proves that depression is not particular about how old its victim is; it, per the devourer behind it all, only seeks to claim another life. And although gender and race are not factors either, there is a substantially greater percentage of females than males who suffer with depression; subsequently, depression is more evident in some ethnicities than in others.[5] Nevertheless, depression (or mental illness) knows no color, no age. It knows no gender and no religion. If these can be the overall statistics, I don't want to imagine how many persons in these groups lived their lives as believers of Jesus Christ.

For the person who deals with mental illness, one of the best things he can do is learn his signs and symptoms and not wait too long before seeking help. Because of the belief system I have for my life, depression did not even cross my mind. It was not considered as a possible cause for why I felt the way I did (and sometimes still do feel). It could never be an option for why I cried. I considered anger. I considered an imbalance of love and support. I considered that I must have sinned. I was convinced that the joy of the Lord was my strength because that was a life lesson instilled into me, and if I didn't feel His joy anymore, then I must have been doing something wrong. Time to call on Jesus.

And while I call on Him, or maybe afterward, I'll also call my counselor and schedule an appointment. Yes, I still pray, but talking to someone who has nothing to lose, or gain for that matter, has been the best medicine for me. I spent so many years not talking, and it turned out to be the key agent in my healing. I can't help but wonder how healthy I could have been had I learned to talk, and trust, well before now. Don't be afraid to seek help. Your consistent sadness, your loss of appetite, your lost desire to do the things you once enjoyed—you're not crazy. You're not unstable. It simply means something has happened in your life, and you've not processed it properly or in a healthy way. But no worries—there's hope! There's help. There's God. There's you.

Ultimately, depression and mental illness has as much power as you give it. Don't allow it to suck the life out of you; rather, you suck the life out it. Smile. Dance. Live.

Walls

*I built this to defend myself
but it has failed to protect myself.*

—Bishop T. D. Jakes

I WAS ABOUT sixteen years old when I decided to not cry anymore. And by the time I was eighteen, I was sure I was not going to cry or ever feel any emotions that had anything to do with sensitivity, vulnerabilities, or any other "ility" there could be if it meant showing anybody that I cared for them or about them. I had learned not to care, and I was good at it. I had grown numb to hurt, and I employed defenses that would ensure no one would hurt me, betray me, or even care for me again. (I began to realize that the pattern of hurt had only come after the sequence of care.) Ensuring no one cared for me or could hurt me would mean I would perhaps have to hurt the other person first. (More on this in the next chapter). Additionally, it meant I had to come up with some type of plan to keep me *in* and to definitely keep other people *out*.

Walls. They would be my tactic of choice as I promptly began to build without even so much of a blueprint as to how thick I wanted them to be, or where I wanted to build them. I just knew I needed protection, walls-of-Jericho-like protection. Joshua 6:1 says that the city of Jericho was so secure that "no one went out and no one came in" (NIV). That was what I needed—effectual security.

And that is what I had for a little while, for about ten years, maybe add another five to ensure there was no premature exposure. And then I had to accept the reality that I was now an adult, and at some point, I would need to trust someone again. If I thought I wanted to love, which I did try at some point during that 10–15 years, I would need to break down walls. If I wanted love in return, I would need to break down walls. If I wanted friends, that meant a breaking down of walls. If I wanted God, I would need to break down walls.

A Moment of Truth

Having this epiphany did not make it any easier for me to cope. I was deadlocked in a conundrum of sorts and was unsure of how or what steps I should take to rid myself of such discontentment. Maybe I should have prayed. Maybe

I should have gone on an extended fast. Perhaps I should have sought counseling, which was a *faux pas* all on its own. But I really did none of these things. Maybe I did pray (a little), but there was not much I could do to be open to tearing down these walls other than to tear down these walls. Change was necessary. And I was reluctant. Like a child acting out in the toy store because she had to settle for the doll with the red hair instead of the one with the blonde, I kicked and I screamed and had an emotional tantrum that was sure to cause God to move the process along much quicker and with as minimal change as possible. Needless to say, He wasn't interested. If I was going to be rid of the walls that I built, then I would need to put in the proper amount of work to tear down the walls that *I* built.

And this would be the moment of truth. I would need to do an assessment of my life, take a look at where I had been, where I was, and where I hoped to go. (There needed to be a point in changing.) And honestly, I was not all too interested in where I hoped to go as much as I was about the fact that I was simply tired. The walls had become inoperative, or maybe they were malfunctioning, and they were no longer operating in their intended purpose. I had been doing all of the work, and soon enough, I was drained. What I had built as protection failed. Perhaps a product of human error, my walls showed me that there is no way to build anything that will last from a temporary situation.

Life Without Walls

It's kind of a scary thought, isn't it? I would be the first to agree with you. I'd also be the first to confess that I have a wall or two still firmly rooted, but no longer built to reach the ceilings of my world. Simply in the event I need a gentle reminder of all of the work I have done to get to the place I am now in my life, a place where I can write about it and hope to help someone else. But I figure if there is the possibility of living a life without limits, even if only in one's imagination, then surely there is the possibility of living a life without walls. Yes, there will be hurt. There will be aches. And there will be pains. People will betray you. People will love you, then leave you (and somehow expect for you not to notice). But a wall-less life, one day at a time, is an attainable goal. I know it may be hard to imagine. It's probably even a much scarier thought to imagine what you will do with the view. Trust me, I know. First comes the shock that there was something on the other side of those walls then there's the emptiness that comes from no longer having those walls. Dilemma: what will you do with the blank canvas of life you now see? Here's an idea. Build something else: a new life. Laugh a little. Don't be afraid to cry a little. (It can actually be a healthier exercise than keeping it all bottled up inside.) Scream if you must. Laugh out loud. Paint a wall red. Dance—in the sunshine *and* in the rain. Kick through the walls. Dance around them like Jacob and company 'til they come tumbling down. Whatever you do, learn to take control over the walls rather than allow them to continue to have control over you. After all, *you* built them.

In all of this, you must remember that every person is different, so every encounter will be different. Someday, you either run out supplies—hurt feelings, damaged emotions, tattered heart, word scars, salty tears—or you get tired of building altogether. At some point though, it may be wise to use those building energies toward another structure: a healthy heart. Otherwise, your walls become not only a means to keep yourself from hurt, but they, by design, become a means for you to hurt others. Needless to say, living with walls does not come without a price. Living without them does not either, but at least, a wall-free life comes with a more affordable price.

Hurt People Hurt People

Pain is no more good when it doesn't hurt anymore.

—Pastor Lamar Simmons

With the idea of walls fresh on the mind, it is befitting to address perhaps the most important reason to break down the emotional, force-field-like protectors erected to secure our forlorn hearts. And that reason is this: hurt people hurt people. The first time I heard this phrase *hurt people hurt people* was quite a few years ago when my pastor said it during a sermon. It was not until the recent months that I have heard this phrase again. First, by Dr. Sandra Wilson (2001)[1], who has written a book whose title bears these words and, even more recently, Pastor Rick Warren (Saddleback Church, California) posted, "Hurt people hurt people" as his status on a social-media website. Either way, written or verbally stated, the repetition of these few words speaks the truth. Hurt people do indeed hurt (other) people.

I encountered Dr. Wilson's book when I was taking a class to complete my requirements for the concentration of my graduate degree. Because I had already begun the composition of the work you now hold in your hand, I chose not to read the book in its entirety as I realized very early on that her book could influence mine. And that was not something I wanted. I wanted my thoughts to be my own, inspired by God, and did not want to produce a duplication of her book. Therefore, I read just enough to complete my assignments. (Surely, I am not the only student guilty of doing this.) Nevertheless, in writing this book, I cannot ignore the validity of Dr. Wilson's (and others') assertion.

I digress as it is not my desire to turn this chapter into a book review. I would rather attempt to capture your attention by inviting you to take a journey down your own memory lane as I give you a glimpse of mine.

In the first part of this book, you read about a few childhood struggles that pretty much set me up to be someone I really did not want to be. By the time I was in high school, I was mean and very rude to even the people I liked. I would often say that it was just me. That was my very *justified* defense, and I dared anyone to dispute it. I was blunt with the truth—or maybe with what was my truth—and if people did not like it, oh well. I responded to people with an attitude as if they had done me wrong. (I guess it was also a way I ensured they wouldn't think to do me wrong.) I was not and have never been a *real* fighter, but I would threaten to push people over the second-floor railings at school. I had a natural reaction to become defensive when someone touched me or if they were too far into my personal space. I was somewhat deranged, to say the least.

All of this behavior had a problem at the root, which I fervently ignored. I was hurt. And maybe this is an issue I did not even know I had until years well into my adult life. Either way, I spent years doing unto others what had been done unto me when I executed an unwarranted sentence upon them.

The funny thing about all of this is when someone would let me know I hurt or offended them—actually, it was more like when I found out, as people were too afraid to admit it themselves—I would apologize and would ensure that that person was not a repeat-victim of my wrath. Yes, I was wrathful. But why? Had the years of being teased (in and outside of the home) been so bottled up in me that my only outlet was to (comically) tell the truth about the other people in the room? Had I been so often rejected that when it would be time for me to reject others, I did it so emphatically that everyone else not only knew of the rejection, but they themselves would also be sure not to inquire anything of me? This only led to more rejection of me. Hurt people hurt people. See how the cycle continues?

Had my emotions been crushed one time too many? Had I been called ugly so much that my self-esteem was nearly diminished completely? To the point where I had to make other people feel ugly? A subconscious effort or not, I was out for blood, seeking revenge on all of the wrong people while attempting to cry out for help—attention—from all the right people (like my mom, my dad, a best friend, people who claimed to care about me).

What's Your Claim to Hurt Fame?

Everybody has one. Or at least every *hurt* person has one. No matter what area of life in which he or she might be struggling, everyone has that something special, that excuse, that reason for why they do what they do, act the way they act. Justification is necessary for defense, and there is nothing no one can do about it. With hands raised, we emphatically declare, "That's just me!" and we dare anyone to dispute our claim to fame.

Perhaps your pain runs deeper than a bad attitude, teasing, or enduring feelings of neglect. Perhaps you have been raped, molested, or something else unthinkable. I have no power to say if any offense is greater than the other. I actually think it is irrational to compare people's pains—no person on the outside looking in can (effectively) tell another person that his or her issue is not that serious or not a big deal. Every *deal* is an individual's own, and he must process it all as he deems necessary. (Although I am sure someone might agree that we don't always process things in a healthy way. But that's not up for discussion at the moment.) Whatever your trophy may be, I dare you to actually own it. Now, of course, that will mean you will actually have to pay attention to yourself. You will have to do a self-evaluation. This should not be too hard after spending so much time evaluating others as you excuse yourself for why you hurt them, and why they were not allowed beyond the wall. You will have to actually look in the mirror, talk to yourself out loud, and be obedient to your heart's desire to not hurt anymore.

"That's easy for you to say." Yes, I hear you. Actually, it's not that easy to say. It is perhaps easier for me to encourage you and tell you to be yourself. If people don't like it, oh well. They'll get over it. And so will you. Or will you? Probably not. I can tell you that as long as you harbor pain that no longer actually hurts, you are doing a disservice to yourself—to your heart and to your life—and to those persons who are waiting to love you, share their life with you, and trusting you to share your love and life with them in return. You've carried the banner long enough. And you have totally outgrown the T-shirt. I get it. It hurts bad. But guess what? You're still here. (And that is a gentle reminder for me.)

I would like to say that it took me *too* long to get to this place in life. I wanted things, *me*, to change, but I was totally reluctant to change. I did not trust the process of friendships, relationships, trust, or love. And, honestly, I still combat these things from time to time. Especially that love part: not the part of loving God and everybody, but the romantic, personal part that invokes vulnerability despite the other person's willingness to also be vulnerable. (Sounds like a wall is still standing firm, huh?) It did not take too long though. I am, I believe, right on target. Too soon, or maybe after this time, and I may have messed up something or someone. And I very well may have shut down on life for good, had I opened up too soon for the wrong person or for the wrong reasons. I don't like the issues I tend to have socially, but God allows everything in its own time for its own reasons. And it is this timing that has caused me to finally take one last look into the trophy case, and take a final walk down the hurt hall of fame so that I may be free of myself and truly live, love, and have the life God intended for me. God did not create us to live alone, but He also did not intend for us to bottle our pain and redistribute it to other people. We have to stop paying so much attention to the hurt in our lives—namely, the past—and allow it to collect dust for a change, rather than polishing it and allowing it to shine every time we reflect on the past. The past should be a reference book, not a dictionary. Let go of the hurt. Stop peeling the scab from the scar. You're already healed. You're already whole. You need only to believe and walk in the truth of God's word.

It takes work, yes. But I did it. So can you.

Get Help

When you are depressed,
waiting until you FEEL like doing what's right
is a huge mistake.
You can't trust your feelings when depressed.

—Pastor Rick Warren

EARLIER YOU READ about my unlikely medicine, more properly known as counseling, and how I was generally in a state of resistance for so long that it has caused me to continue sessions for more than a year now. I am not so sure if that speaks of how bad off I really was, or if it simply shows how reluctant I was, and still sometimes am, to change. Ultimately, at least in my very personal opinion, it was a matter of not sharing my business. For the most part, I am a fairly private person. I hardly share things with friends and family, much less some counselor. I guess my "business" is out now if you are holding this book in your hands. But I realize too that maybe, if I had started talking years ago, there would not have been so much unhealthy thinking that needed to be undone. And maybe I could spend every other Thursday afternoon doing something else.

Consider the Options

Complain, check. Cry, check. Pray, check. Fast, check. Go to work, go to church with a smile, check. Now what? You're at home now. You're alone now. You break down now. Again *now*. You have done all you know how to do from talking to God, family, and trusted companions to any variation of these things listed above. And you've probably tried some unconventional, unhealthy options too, like excessive alcohol consumption, taking one pill too many, overeating, undereating just to name a few. With these possible resorts in mind, I suppose I should be a bit more spiritual at some point. *Spirituality* should lead me to ask you if you have tried Jesus while, or better yet, instead of, trying all of these other things. I'm sorry. This is not *that* book. I trust that you have tried Jesus. But if you haven't, you can try Him even in this moment. But this book, by default, is not a call to salvation. Rather, it is a call to life. So perhaps, in that regard, it is a call to salvation. But how do you get there?

I would probably be among the group of people who would, without hesitation, ask a person if she has prayed about the situation she has come to me to talk about. And, of course, there are the enthusiasts among us who emphatically cast out scriptures as if they were stones being cast by he who has no sin if a person were to dare mention that she has resorted to other means of "healing" than that which is conducive to *church* liturgy that employs *only* faith, fasting, and prayer as the acceptable process for she who is in need of healing. These ideas are perhaps often misunderstood rites of faith. And for the person who does honestly believe in God and His power to heal, this route to healing could breed misconception, and thereby contempt, because he was sick and in need of healing, but did not consider all of the options to obtain that healing.

In my days of neglect, denial, or whatever anyone would like to call it, one of the best pieces of advice was from my pastor when he told me that spiritual consultation is good, but it's okay to seek professional counseling outside of the church. Perhaps that was the *okay* I needed to not feel like I was betraying my faith and my belief in God. I mean, I had to face it: the usual resolves I had for coping were really not working anymore. They had no power because I had grown accustomed to the cycle—shutdown, withdraw, write about it, suffer silently, and all the while make sure I keep a smile on my face, so no one would think to inquire about what might be wrong. What else did I (really) have to lose? I had grown weary of my normal options, and at least by (finally) trying something else, I could have an excuse when that too seemed to not work.

I became more accepting of the options when, during worship service one day, my pastor said that God heals in two ways: by miracle or by medicine. That is an idea I have shared when talking with other people, so I believe it is only befitting to share that thought with you as I make an effort to list a few options for you to consider as you trek your path to healing, wholeness, and a continued state of peace. These ideas are not listed in any particular order of suggestion. I extend this disclaimer because you will see that I did not list a "God-solution" first. I know I perhaps should have, considering my background. But let's face it: how many of us, and how often do we, actually turn to God before trying everything else or talking to anyone else first? I would like to think God is *always* my first resolve, but the truth of the matter is He isn't. Sometimes I resort to nothing at all. At least that way, I can only be upset with myself when things don't change.

With that in mind, let us proceed. This list is definitely not conclusive. I am mainly suggesting a few general options that have either been suggested to me, or that I have even tried for myself. Mental health counseling, medication, spiritual and/or religious beliefs or practices, meditation, and relaxation are all things suggested by associates, coworkers, fellow soldiers, the counselor, a social worker, the pastor. Of course, my list of other negative, and perhaps very unhealthy, options is a bit longer than this. But we're all about getting better not getting (or staying) worse. Isn't it interesting that there are more unhealthy choices than there are healthy ones? No wonder, it is sometimes so easy to give in. But we're not doing that this time.

Mental Health Counseling

Even though we may want to ignore it, we must consider the notion that God has given us doctors, counselors, social workers, mental health providers, or whatever we may choose to call them, because He knew that there would be a need for them. Contrary to what the radical, charismatic faith movement may have taught us, none of these professions are limited to the secular world, the unbeliever, the sinner, or whatever category with which we make an effort to ensure no association. As I have stated elsewhere in this book, Christianity, faith in God, or whatever, does not negate human suffering. Seek help. If you need someone to talk to other than God, seek help. (I'm sure I may get stoned for that statement. But surely, I'm not the only one who has felt like God wasn't listening or just felt like she needed a real-life human being with whom to communicate.) Reach out to social services and/or other providers in your area, like not-for-profit organizations that offer free or perhaps low-cost services. These people have gone to school, practiced many hours, and taken on the cases of other people just like you—just like us. They are waiting to be the unbiased, listening ear that you have been longing for. Oh, I know the feeling. Sometimes we just need someone who will just listen. Seek the assistance of these professionals in your church, in your community, in your city, and in your state. Find that 800 number. Call a hotline. Phone a friend. Consider the options.

Medication

Although I have not always been open to it—and it is still *not* my favorite thing to do—talking to someone has perhaps been the best medicine for me. Talking to God is cool, but according to Genesis 2, even He thinks it is necessary for us to have at least one other human being with whom to relate. So, counseling has been my medication. The thing about counseling though is the possibility of the counselor or social worker suggesting other things to help you cope for when you're not in her office on that couch, or sitting in the chair, which is my preferred stance as I mete out my fears and deepest emotions. My counselor has not suggested medication, but there was one time when my usual counselor was unavailable. I was given the option of going to another facility. I typically would not have chosen to talk with someone different or new, but I had had a major episode—PTSD-type episode—and because I had worked so hard in my sessions up to that point, I felt the need to address the incident quickly.

So I went to have a chat with the alternative. She was familiar with my counselor and praised her enough for me to find myself more confident in *my* counselor's ability. Mrs. Social Worker listened to me, asked me questions—please don't ask me about my childhood—and stated her diagnosis: PTSD. But it was only "mild." She further concluded that I was suffering from depression and inquired if I would be interested in taking medication. She didn't quite ask so directly. It was more like, "have you considered?" I quickly said I hadn't and rejected her suggestion even quicker. She was certain it would help. I was certain I didn't really care to be in her office in the first place, so I definitely didn't need anything else adding to the shifty diagnoses of crazy.

But is medication really that bad? I mean, if it is really something that can minimize anxiety and all other emotions that come with depression, it may not be too bad after all. However—of course, there's a however—like any other medications, a person must be mindful of the side effects. Antidepressants are the most common medications prescribed to persons dealing with depression. Aside from the fact that I just don't want to have to take them, it makes me nervous to know that scientists don't really know how antidepressants work.[1] I guess it simply matters that they do something to the brain that causes a person to feel happy (or happier). At any rate, if you decide to take antidepressants, it is suggested that you allow time for them to work as it could take weeks before you see any full results.[2] Additionally, you should not discontinue your medication unless told to do so by your doctor. (And that rules me out right there. I am typically never faithful to take medication, and if I do take any, I readily stop taking it whenever I want.) And if you're like me, once you learn of the possible side effects to be experienced from using these drugs, you will much rather deal with your issues on your own and without any drugs at all. We all may agree that we have enough problems without such an addition. Nevertheless, we may agree that sometimes we simply want to feel better quickly and on a more consistent basis so that we can get back to living our lives.

I have rejected the social worker's suggestion for medication and intend to do so if the opportunity presents itself again. It is my personal choice, and a decision I had to make on my own. Besides, if I need a pick-me-up, I can always count on a cold cup of mocha-latte whatever from that favored coffee shop, like the one a friend bought for me one day, to send me straight to the moon. (I was so high, I don't think I'll try that drink again. Coffee is not for the fainthearted.) Just know which options are available to you, as there are many antidepressants and other alternatives that can be prescribed to you to help you cope. You're not alone, and God will not be mad with you for your choice. God heals by miracle and by medicine. Consider the options.

Spiritual and/or Religious Affiliation

Don't worry and don't clinch up on me now. This is *not* the part where I command you to make your way to the altar, lift your hands, and make Jesus your personal Lord and Savior. This is not an altar call or any of the sort. This is simply a notation of an option that you could consider to help yourself be a better, healthier self. I'm not saying having some level of spirituality or religious belief system is the end-all, be-all for a life of peace. If that were the case, I would have had no just cause to pen this book because, if nothing else, I ascribe to spirituality, as I believe it is necessary to have a connection with something outside of the self, on a deeper level. In my case, it is God.

When performing research during my graduate studies, I learned, or maybe it was simply confirmed, that people who insert some level of spirituality into their personal and family life find that they have a greater resilience to life's not-so-favorable circumstances. Did all the people in these studies believe in or serve the same God? No. I suppose the gist is that they believed in and had faith in an entity outside of themselves, one which they believe is greater than they are. And having this belief in something outside of themselves gives them a serene resolve inwardly. There is a peace that comes from trusting that you are not alone, and there is a God with the power to relieve you of your burdens. Perhaps you trust the philosophies of Buddha or Confucius. Maybe you reverence the teachings of Muhammad. Maybe, for you, God is in some way in the stars or in nature. Maybe God, or the idea of Him—the Christian God or any other—is not even real for you. But what if spirituality, becoming one with the self, God, the gods, or whatever, is actually a means by which you can achieve peace? The saying goes, "don't knock it till you try it."

Because I am a Christian, and because the book is written from my experience as such, I would be remiss if I didn't suggest you give God—Jesus Christ—a try. He's definitely worth it. Consider the opinions.

Meditation

In his letter to the Philippian church, Paul writes, "Finally, brethren, whatsoever things are true, whatsoever things are honest, whatsoever things are just, whatsoever things are pure, whatsoever things are lovely, whatsoever things are of good report; if there be any virtue, and if there be any praise, think on these things" (Phil. 4:8). This only gets easier over time and with much practice. And when depressed, I know we want to think of the lie rather than the truth, the dishonest thing rather than the honest, the unjust rather the just, the impure, the unlovely, the not-so-good report. Sometimes we want to feel better and just can't seem to get the proper grip. Other times though, I know we want to stay right where we are and wallow in our pity, or cry those tears, or stay in the bed with the blinds closed. We want to endure the sadness because we have more than convinced ourselves that even if happiness chooses to show its face, it'll soon depart and leave none of itself behind. Sadness will come again. So I get it—if I'm going to be sad anyway, I may as well stay sad.

But maybe I can convince you, Elijah, to come from under the juniper tree for just a moment. Instead of lying there meditating on giving up, dying, and all other self-demising plots, think of the good times, the happy times, the better times. Even if you feel you've not had any of those better times, I challenge you to think long enough until you remember. Remember how it was before you were called ugly and your self-esteem was damaged. Remember how you felt when that trusted someone lovingly held you in his or her arms *before* he tainted your body and robbed you of your innocence. Remember what it felt like to laugh a good laugh from the gut. Remember what it was that made you laugh. Remember what it felt like to love before your heart was broken, before your trust was betrayed. Think happy thoughts.

Concentrate on the Word of God and all of the great things it has to say about you. Meditate on those things. Take out your journal and write. Be honest with the person in the room, *you*. Think about how it could be if you chose to smile again and do so more consistently. What if you chose to sing again, laugh out loud again, love again, live again? How much healthier could you be in your heart, in your mind? How much more will you want to be around people, and people want to be around you? The enemy comes to attack our thoughts because he typically doesn't have much power to do much of anything else. He believes, however, that if he can get control over your mind, he will have control over your actions. If he can get you to believe no one cares about you, not even God, then he knows pretty soon, he'll have himself another victim who has fallen prey.

In the army, I learned that the challenges we faced were first mental, then physical. Of course it hardly felt that way, but I eventually learned that my success in basic training and my future army life would be an instance of mind over matter. It was much easier to adapt to this reasoning in the army than it was in my real life, but I can appreciate the principle. Perhaps Paul was really on to something. So take Paul's advice and think on those things that are much better than the negative things to which you've already given so much thought. Consider the options.

"[B]ut be ye transformed by the renewing of your mind…" (Rom. 12:2).

Relaxation

David said, "He maketh me to lie down in green pastures…" (Ps. 23:2). Jesus said, "Come unto me, all ye that labour and are heavy laden, and I will give you rest" (Matt. 11:28). God, who has all power, deemed it necessary to take a day of rest. I have no clue why people, me included, believe that we do not need to take time to simply rest. Chill out. Take a day off to do absolutely *nothing*. It was not until one too many things happened, and I was out of work for more than a few months that I decided to (finally) give in to rest's call. My body had been craving for it. My spirit had been in dire need of it, but I was convinced that I had things I needed to do, and they must be done now or as quickly after now as possible. There was no time to waste, and there was no need to rest until something had been accomplished. My mind and spirit would teach me otherwise, and I would eventually lose the battle and find myself in a state of rest. Now there's almost nothing that can take me from it, and it has become my emphatic, declarative piece of advice I share when people choose to confide in me: take some time to rest.

And by rest, I simply mean take time to do what you love or do nothing at all. Take a day off from work. Take a day off from church. I was surprised at the relief I had just from missing a Sunday service, not because I had to work, but simply to stay at home. I may have watched a worship service online, but I'm sure I purposely overslept. I may have even cleaned up my home a bit, but I didn't work hard, and I didn't leave the house. I rested. One of the biggest lessons I've learned over the last ten years is that I must simply take time for myself. Because I'm very analytical, I am always thinking. And because I care so much about people, I'm always considering what I can do for someone else. I realize taking time to think about things may be a profitable asset, but spending too much time thinking about those things can eventually cause concern, worry, and unnecessary stress.

Taking rest does not particularly mean you're being lazy. (It took a while for me to comprehend that concept.) It simply means you are taking time for yourself, taking time away from the stressors of life—work, school, church, family, or whatever causes you stress—and taking a moment to regroup, to recuperate so that you may consistently be the best *you* you have to offer. (And in case you were wondering, one definition for the word *recuperate* is "to regain a former state or condition; especially to recover health or strength," as defined by *Merriam-Webster*.) People will drain you. Work can drain you. Situations and circumstances can drain you. And unless you have the ability to retreat and consider yourself (for a change), you will perhaps always find yourself stuck in a forty-year cycle of wilderness wandering and never reach the Promised Land. Trust me—you don't want God to have to make you rest. So slow down, take your time. Take your rest. God chooses not to slumber in order to make sure you can. Consider the options.

As aforementioned, these options are not the only (healthy) ones that may be available to you. They are just the alternatives that have been accessible to me, in addition to all of the constricted "church" options or responses to which I have been limited for many years. Don't get me wrong—prayer still works, and God absolutely has the power to heal us of all sickness and manners of disease. However, it does not negate the fact that He has various ways by which we are able to experience His healing power. Before giving in to the temptation of the unhealthy options, before completely giving up, please, *please* consider the options.

The Choice is Yours

Let's consider the following:

> Now there is at Jerusalem by the sheep market a pool, which is called in the Hebrew tongue Bethesda,

having five porches. In these lay a great multitude of impotent folk, of blind, halt, withered, waiting for the moving of the water. For an angel went down at a certain season into the pool, and troubled the water: whosoever then first after the troubling of the water stepped in was made whole of whatsoever disease he had. And a certain man was there, which had an infirmity thirty and eight years. When Jesus saw him lie, and knew that he had been now a long time in that case, he saith unto him, Wilt thou be made whole? The impotent man answered him, Sir, I have no man, when the water is troubled, to put me into the pool: but while I am coming, another steppeth down before me. Jesus saith unto him, Rise, take up thy bed, and walk. And immediately the man was made whole... (John 5:2–9)

Here, there is a man who has been lame for thirty-eight years. He was pretty accustomed to his condition and perhaps quite comfortable as it is obvious that he stayed *near* the pool, but never made his way *into* the pool so that he may encounter healing. I highlighted the latter part of verse seven because it offers what the man believes is a valid response for his condition. (Notice, however, that Jesus never asked about the pool or why the man had not been healed; He simply asked the man if he wanted to be healed, made whole.) It is interesting that he identified with something that wasn't even the problem, as if to say, if it wasn't for the other people jumping in before me, I'd already be healed. Jesus's inquiry required a response of faith and a desire for change. And so it is, or perhaps it even goes without saying that the choice to be healed is absolutely up to the individual in need of healing. The choice to experience something different, something new, to have peace, to live life is completely up to you. I suppose it is all a matter of personal desire. What do *you* want? Do you want to be made whole? Will you be like this man and offer excuses or make a decision to answer yes or no? The choice, again, is yours and yours alone. (Not even Jesus could choose for this man, and He can't and won't choose for you.)

Let's consider another example:

> And it came to pass on a certain day, as he was teaching, that there were Pharisees and doctors of the law sitting by, which were come out of every town of Galilee, and Judaea, and Jerusalem: and the power of the Lord was present to heal them. And, behold, men brought in a bed a man which was taken with a palsy: and they sought means to bring him in, and to lay him before him.
>
> And when they could not find by what way they might bring him in because of the multitude, they

went upon the housetop, and let him down through the tiling with his couch into the midst before Jesus. And when he saw their faith, he said unto him, Man, thy sins are forgiven thee. (Luke 5:17–20)

Now I can appreciate not only the paralyzed man in this passage, but also his friends. (This idea is perhaps a whole other message and a chapter in and of itself. But how much more enhanced could our lives be if we simply had better friends?) Sometimes we need someone in our corner who will not only sit and cry with us, sit and listen to us complain, or sit and criticize us like Job's three dear friends did with and to him. But we also need friends who will take action when we do not have the ability or strength to do so for ourselves. I cannot accept the idea that it was simply the faith of the man with palsy that made him whole, but it was also the faith of his friends. I digress because, all that aside, this man *allowed* his friends to carry him into the healing service that was taking place. He *chose* to be carried because he had a desire to be healed. Like this man, the choice is yours.

There are other scenarios in the Bible that highlight the faith of every person who was healed or made whole or delivered from demonic possession or depression or whatever the ailment may have been. Some things take prayer and fasting (and of course, you can apply these to all things). Prayer should be employed in every matter. And it takes faith—period—to even believe healing can take place no matter what the sickness, ailment, issue, or disease may be. The woman with the issue of blood: she made a choice. Jarius on behalf of his daughter: he made a choice. David in the Cave of Adullam: he made a choice. King Hezekiah in the face of sickness and death: he made a choice. Elijah under the juniper tree: albeit reluctantly, he made a choice. Jesus in the Garden of Gethsemane: He made a choice. Why do I mention these few examples? Because they are examples of the variance of need people may have. From physical sickness to mental distresses, faith in action—desire for change—is the necessary agent for deliverance. But, in all circumstances, you mustn't forget that the choice is yours.

With all of that said, what will you do to help yourself? You've tried to cope on your own. And how's that working out for you? If you're anything like me, once you get tired enough, you will make a conscious decision to change and employ available resources to help you reach that goal. I would not dare tell you that it doesn't take work. It is a matter of consistent consciousness to choose peace over chaos, joy over sadness. There are series of days when it is a struggle every day. Then there are days when everything is fine. Either way, it is a decision, a choice, a desire for change that has to be decided on the part of the person who is suffering. In the context of this book, stability and peace is an adequate desire and perhaps the primary one. If you trust the Word of God that He will keep you in perfect peace if you keep your mind on Him (see Isaiah 26:3), then work toward that every day and don't give up on yourself just because it seems to take longer than you hoped.

This is the jumpstart to wholeness, but I encourage you to not stop here. I don't believe in medications, because a person can become dependent on them. This is *my* personal choice. I do, however, encourage you to use your resources—talk to someone, go to counseling, pray, exercise regularly, change your environment, change your friends, but most of all, *change your mind*. Don't be embarrassed by your need to get help from someone other than your pastor and someplace other than your church. If you take medication, seek to be independent of it—take it one day at a time until you don't have to need it anymore. Seek more natural resolves like quiet time, peaceful walks, or journal writing. I know I choose to even bake sometimes. And I've read a few self-help books and listened to a lot of music. But I have not obtained my current state of mind on my own. I gave in to seeking help. Fear can be binding, but try your best to boycott it and seek help. Your health—your life—depends on it.

*I've learned this:
It only takes a moment to hurt,
or be hurt,
but it could take years to heal from that moment…
Don't let anyone rush your process—
it's different for us all.
The important thing is that you heal
and heal well—
I need you to survive.*

Remember the Word

Depression is a body, soul, and spirit problem
that requires a balanced body, soul, and spirit answer.

—Neil T. Anderson, *The Bondage Breaker*

IN REGARDS TO considering the options, perhaps the most important is this: *remember the Word*. And by Word, I mean the Word of God. This is not simply a matter of you remembering to rehearse verses you have labeled as anecdotes sure to send your faith into a frenzy and invoke pretentious hope. You know what I mean. They are the words we conjure when we need motivation to get through, or encourage others while they are going through, the not-so-favorable times in life. Like "life and death are in the power of the tongue," or "all things work together for the good to them who love God," or "call those things which be not as though they were," which is generally misinterpreted; but that's a discussion for another book. At any rate, we have somehow managed to limit ourselves to what I'll call "feel good" scriptures, and we forget about the rest of the Bible. However, if we were to read in the Bible where the enemy made a personal appearance to tempt his prey, he did not exactly quote any of our favorites. He didn't repeat what Moses said or what Paul said, but he did repeat, albeit slightly altered, what God said. In Eden or in the wilderness, the enemy used the Word of God as the key weapon in his arsenal of temptation.

So if the enemy employs this secret as a means for defeat in our lives, how much more should we do the same so that we may have major success and victory in our own lives? This, I believe, is the only time I would ever suggest that a person follow the enemy's lead. Otherwise, never, ever consider following in his footsteps, for he'll surely lead you into death. Still, how is it possible for the enemy to believe in the Word of God more than we do? (And the Word was written *for* us!)

There's not too much I can say here that has not perhaps been said already in so many other words. But, as you near the end of this book, I can only hope that you have been able to find something in it profitable for your life. Even still, there is nothing that I could have said in the previous chapters, or the few that are to follow this one, that are more important than the Word of God, the Scriptures, the Holy Bible, the Good Book—whatever it is you want to call it. It contains solutions to life's problems and, more specifically, the problems of the spirit.

Focus on what it is the Bible has to say about you. "'For I know the plans I have for you,' declares the LORD, 'plans to prosper you and not to harm you, plans to give you hope and a future'" (Jer. 29:11, NIV). "But he knoweth the way that I take: when he hath tried me, I shall come forth as gold" (Job 23:10). "But those who hope in the Lord will renew their strength. They will soar on wings like eagles; they will run and not grow weary, they will walk and not be faint" (Isa. 40:31, NIV). These are affirmations to remember and ammunitions to have in your arsenal to defeat the enemy (and oftentimes the self). And, of course, there are many more noteworthy passages that aren't mentioned here; so feel free to establish your own favorites, verses that are particularly on reserve for you to encourage yourself as you will. Remembering the Word will invoke encouragement every time, and you will find yourself with just a little more strength for your journey of life. So, whatever you do—before giving up, before walking away, before quitting, before taking one too many pills, before going through with the suicide attempt—choose to, there's that word again, *choose* to remember the Word.

You have to believe you can
before you will.
For some, your biggest battle
will take place within the confines of your mind.
You will be your biggest enemy.
Allowing fear, doubt, confusion or paranoia
to consume your energy is a guaranteed way
to halt progress.
The longer you dwell on a thing,
the larger it becomes.
If you want to see a positive change,
begin with your thoughts,
couple them with action
and watch everything else begin to follow suit…

—Teira E. Farley

Shower, Shave, and Change

There's too much life wrapped in your voice—
you've got to get up from here.

—"Gilda" in *For Colored Girls*

THERE IS PERHAPS no simpler way to express the sentiments of this chapter. Like in the rest of the book, or at least this section, this chapter will serve as your invocation to change. Besides, what more is there to say? You have gotten a glimpse into my silent world; you have been bombarded with biblical passages, lofty anecdotes, inspiring quotes, and one or two statistics. What else do you need? You're good to go, right? Perhaps I should send you on your way trusting that what you have read so far is sufficient enough for the next chapter of your life's journey. Or I can tell you this: now that you've decided to change, it is time that you actually make a change.

The Request of the King

If you really need a reason to get out of bed, open the blinds, brush your teeth, comb your hair, take a shower, change your clothes, or simply smile for a change, what can be better than actually being beckoned by the king? Check this out:

> And it came to pass in the morning that his spirit was troubled; and he sent and called for all the magicians of Egypt, and all the wise men thereof: and Pharaoh told them his dream; but there was none that could interpret them unto Pharaoh…And there was there with us a young man, an Hebrew, servant to the captain of the guard; and we told him, and he interpreted to us our dreams; to each man according to his dream he did interpret. And it came to pass, as he interpreted to us, so it was; me he restored unto mine office, and him he hanged.
>
> Then Pharaoh sent and called Joseph, and they brought him hastily out of the dungeon: and he shaved himself, and changed his raiment, and came in unto Pharaoh. (Gen. 41:8, 12–14)

It can be assumed that Joseph did not know exactly why the king was requesting his presence. It is easy enough to say he was waiting to be called, but truth is, Joseph had somewhat fallen into a state of depression concerning his once hopeful release from prison. He thought the butler would remember him, but he didn't. At least not until two years later.

It is interesting to me though that Joseph could be in some state of depression but still be mindful enough of who was requesting his presence. He believed the call so much that he did not question if it was really the king calling. He did not inquire if it was a joke. He simply—and immediately—made a change. He cleaned himself, changed his clothes and then made his appearance.

So what will it take for you to make that change? Are you waiting to receive a call from the president (of the United States or otherwise)? Are you going to allow your depression to get the best of who you are and consume your life? Later in the passage of scripture above, the text says that the king had heard about Joseph and his ability to interpret dreams (v. 15). We don't know what all Joseph did during that period between being forgotten and then remembered by the butler. His appearance, though, suggests that he was at least tired of waiting and was prepared for another day of the same thing. I know I've been there—tired of waiting for things to change, accepting depression, unhappiness, confusion, and fear as my definitive *normal*. The butler, my mother, my father, my friends, anyone, had forgotten about me, and I must live this life of bondage, enslaved to the instability of my mind.

And then the day comes—or it shall come—when your name is called. It may not be through the mode of which you might prefer, but I encourage you to listen for your name. My name was called the day I realized I had spent one day too many in the bed with my blinds closed. My name was called the day I learned of another Christian who had chosen to commit suicide. I hear my name with every word I write or with every response I get from someone who reads the words I write. And my presence is requested for no other reason than this: to live. That is what Joseph was waiting for; that is why Joseph shaved and changed his clothes. He simply wanted an opportunity to live, live free, and become what he had seen in his own dreams so many years before. So what will you do when your name is called?

I must, again, echo the words of Gilda, "There's too much life wrapped in your voice—you've got to get up from here."

*When our heart belongs to God,
the world and its powers
cannot steal it from us.*

—Henri J. M. Nouwen, *Reaching Out*

Rest in Peace Now[1]

And as you lay there in your blood I said to you, "Live!"
—Ezekiel 16:6, NIV

SEEMS LIKE A farfetched idea. I know, but let me explain.
Two days ago made a year since my young friend and brother in Christ, Davonn Brewton[2], sustained a gunshot wound that would lead to his last breath. I can remember the moment in which I received the news. It was late on a Saturday night, and my insistent insomnia had me perusing television channels and a social network simultaneously. I couldn't believe what I was reading as I scrolled down the news feed. The post of a family friend was the first I saw. I clicked on the pages of various other family and friends. Their updates were consistent. However, I still did not—could not—believe it. Duke, as he was affectionately called, was *dead*.

I would not be satisfied with this news for quite some time, although, I did finally make an attempt to face reality after receiving further confirmation from my mom via text message. The week leading up to his homegoing service was a nostalgic one. I still couldn't believe he was gone. Someone took his life from him. He was only twenty-one years old. He had so much more life to live, and now he laid there cold in a pearl-colored box numb to the passersby who bid him farewell.

Although they've never been my favorite thing to attend anyway, I took a break from attending funerals after that. All the deaths I had learned of prior to his, and all of the funerals I had attended for family or in ministerial service had not prepared me to say goodbye to this young friend. Duke's death, if nothing else, put things in perspective for me. After many tears, I had to encourage myself that God does all things well and doesn't make mistakes. For the first time, I could remember, I wanted to question God about death. I wondered if Duke had enough time in his final moments to ensure his status with God. I wondered why God would let it happen like this. May Duke rest in peace.

Duke's death, at the very least, reaffirmed this one thing: life is short. Even if someone makes it to see a hundred years old, life is short. Even more than that, I have come to understand in greater detail that I never know when my time will be up on this earth, so I must do my best to live. Like, should I, really, have to die before I *rest in peace*?

As I remember Duke, I think of a classmate who was recently laid to rest. A classmate, thirty-two years old. Stunned at the news, I realized that I was still praying the same thing I had prayed a year ago: Lord, help me to live. I don't know why I have such a hard time with this, and why I cannot seem to fully grasp the concept of living a full life (and doing so out loud). Although death puts things in perspective every time I learn of it, it seems the effects wear off one moment too soon, and I need another dose of bad news. But it really should not have to be this way. My life isn't so bad that I have to choose whether or not I will be happy or sad on any given day. The fact that I am alive is a reason to smile, for it could have surely been another way.

So, in memory of Davonn "Prince Duke" Brewton, and those who passed before him—Grandma Battle, Goddaddy Mance, Brother Ron—I rededicate my life to living. In the book of Isaiah, believers are encouraged that God will keep a man in perfect peace if he keeps his mind on God (see Isaiah 26:3). And the Apostle Paul encourages believers to "live in peace and the God of love and peace" will be with them (see 2 Corinthians 13:11). The possibility of resting in peace, living in peace, is great. Not every day of my life has to be a chaotic one. I must choose to rest in peace. And I know it doesn't always happen. I have many sleepless and restless nights, but to know that the possibility of peace can be my reality before I take my *final* rest encourages me to live life more fully. I hope you too can find the bright side to life *and living*, even if you only see it as the opposite of death.

A Eulogy

It is interesting that such a distinct word of encouragement, rest in peace, is said to a man after he can no longer hear it. Even in death, a man is given a charge to keep—and because he is now *resting*—friends and loved ones trust that he won't fail. But why must a person have to wait until he or she dies to experience such rest? Is not rest attainable now—while breathing, *living*? Jesus said, "I am come that they might have life, and that they might have it more abundantly" (John 10:10). Now I could be wrong, but I am fairly certain that Jesus was *not* talking about the afterlife or life in heaven. He was talking about having a full life while here on the earth. He was talking about having the best life *now*. He was talking about resting in peace *now*.

This concept has taken some time for me to grasp. Not because it is such a far-fetched idea, but simply because it is an idea that was not presented to me this way. Being a believer is so much more than what we make it. It is so much more than making the (sometimes forced) decision about our final destination—choosing *now* between heaven and hell. I spent many years believing that I must gruelingly endure the pressures of this life, and simply life itself, while at the same time trusting that I'll fly away some glad morning when this life is over. Or holding on to the hope that soon I will be done with the troubles of this world, as I firmly protest that nobody knows the troubles I see. But someone does know. Jesus knew, for we have not an high priest which cannot be touched with the feeling of our infirmities (see Hebrews 4:15). Other people, believers and nonbelievers alike, know (even if they are too embarrassed to share their story). And, as you have read, I also know. The troubles you see, the troubles you feel, the troubles you fear you'll someday see and feel—God knows. You are not alone in your life and *you can choose* to have the best life now, the best peace now. You can rest well now. You can live *now*!

Why wait for the moment when you can no longer enjoy it, when people are crying and singing over you, and speaking words that you cannot hear? Rest now. There is a Sabbath for a reason; therefore, no matter what day it is you are now reading these words, make today that Sabbath day. Take your rest and rest in peace. This is the charge I make to you (and myself) in life, so when death does come, we can surely take our rest and have no qualms about how to do it—we'll transition peacefully without regret.

My friend, go and take your rest.

*Most folks are about as happy as they
make up their minds to be.*

—Abraham Lincoln

In God's garden of grace, even a broken tree bears fruit.
—Brother Matthew Warren

Notes

A Silent Epidemic

1. "Depression." NIMH RSS. Accessed April 1, 2014. http://www.nimh.nih.gov/health/topics/depression.
2. See note 1.
3. "Ten Leading Causes of Death and Injury." Centers for Disease Control and Prevention. March 31, 2015. Accessed April 9, 2015. http://www.cdc.gov/injury/wisqars/leadingcauses.html
4. See note 3.
5. See note 1.

Hurt People Hurt People

1. Wilson, Sandra D. *Hurt People Hurt People: Hope & Healing for Yourself and Your Relationships.* Grand Rapids, MI: Discovery House, 2001.

Get Help

1. See note 1.
2. See note 1.

Rest in Peace Now

1. Gilbert, Liconya. "Rest in Peace… Now?" Church Girl Chronicles. August 27, 2013. Accessed March 1, 2014. http://churchgirlchronicles.blogspot.com/.
   Original title published as a blog post to churchgirlchronicles.blogspot.com. Additional text has been added for the purposes of this book.
2. In memory of Davonn "Prince Duke" Brewton, Sr. 1991–2012, another victim of gun violence.